Start Your Own

COACHING
BUSINESS

Additional titles in *Entrepreneur's Startup Series*

Start Your Own

Arts and Crafts Business
Automobile Detailing Business
Bar and Club
Bed and Breakfast
Blogging Business
Business on eBay
Car Wash
Child-Care Service
Cleaning Service
Clothing Store and More
Coaching Business
Coin-Operated Laundry
Construction and Contracting Business
Consulting Business
Day Spa and More
e-Business
Event Planning Business
Executive Recruiting Business
Fashion Accessories Business
Florist Shop and Other Floral Businesses
Food Truck Business
Freelance Writing Business and More
Freight Brokerage Business
Gift Basket Service
Grant-Writing Business
Graphic Design Business
Green Business

Hair Salon and Day Spa
Home Inspection Service
Import/Export Business
Information Marketing Business
Kid-Focused Business
Lawn Care or Landscaping Business
Mail Order Business
Medical Claims Billing Service
Net Services Business
Online Education Business
Personal Concierge Service
Personal Training Business
Pet Business and More
Pet-Sitting Business and More
Photography Business
Public Relations Business
Restaurant and More
Retail Business and More
Self-Publishing Business
Seminar Production Business
Senior Services Business
Travel Business and More
Tutoring and Test Prep Business
Vending Business
Wedding Consultant Business
Wholesale Distribution Business

Entrepreneur MAGAZINE'S

startup

Start Your Own

2ND EDITION

COACHING BUSINESS

Your Step-by-Step Guide to Success

Entrepreneur Press and Monroe Mann
Revised by Rich Mintzer

EP
Entrepreneur PRESS®

Entrepreneur Press, Publisher
Cover Design: Beth Hansen-Winter
Production and Composition: Eliot House Productions

This publication is designed to provide accurate and authoritative information in regard to the subject matter covered. It is sold with the understanding that the publisher is not engaged in rendering legal, accounting or other professional services. If legal advice or other expert assistance is required, the services of a competent professional person should be sought.

Library of Congress Cataloging-in-Publication Data
    Mintzer, Richard.
      Start your own coaching business / by Entrepreneur Press and Richard Mintzer.—2nd ed.
        p.   cm.
      Rev. ed. of: Start your own coaching business / Entrepreneur Press and Monroe Mann. c2008.
      Includes index.
      ISBN-13: 978-1-59918-445-6 (alk. paper)
      ISBN-10: 1-59918-445-1 (alk. paper)
        1. Personal coaching—Handbooks, manuals, etc. 2. New business enterprises—Handbooks, manuals, etc. I. Mann, Monroe. Start your own coaching business. II. Entrepreneur Press. III. Title.
    BF637.P36M35 2012
    158.3068'1—dc23   2012024250

Printed in the United States of America

16 15 14 13 12   10 9 8 7 6 5 4 3 2 1

Contents

▲

Chapter 9

Profit and Loss 65

Chapter 10

Running Your Business. 73

Chapter 11

Improving Your Offerings 79

Preface

The appeal of becoming a motivational coach is greater today than ever before. With that in mind, this book is written for the many people who want to become motivational coaches and run their own coaching business.

It is for those who want to hone their coaching skills and help others reach their goals. It is written expressly for those who want to work hands-on, one-on-one with their clients to help them think bigger, and become more successful.

Originally, this book was written by Monroe Mann, who started his own coaching business from the ground up and spent seven years at the grass roots level learning the business through trial and error. During that time he also served his country for 18 months in Iraq. (More about Monroe is in the back of the book.)

As Mann puts it, "It is the result of falling on my face time and time again, and making hundreds of mistakes with my own company, Unstoppable Artists—a company I started from the ground up on a shoestring budget in 2001 and is today a premier business, marketing, and financial coaching firm for those in show business, music, and publishing."

While Mann has taken on the practical coaching of people in show business, you can find your own niche or appeal to a broad market. The choice is yours.

In this, the updated version of this coaching business primer, you can get an understanding of what it takes to train and hone your skills before setting yourself up as a coach, hopefully minimizing the pitfalls along the way.

The objective of this book is to explain what you need to know to get started, how to properly position yourself, how to handle both the internal and external aspects of running the business, and even what to do when you want to expand.

Here, we take a long-term approach and assume that you are considering starting a motivational coaching firm. We explain how to start such a business, how to expand it, sell it or even franchise it down the road. You can then understand exactly where the company can go, even if you decide not to take it there.

There are only three things this book can't provide you: the discipline, the guts, and the enthusiasm to take the plunge, train to become a coach and start out in business, which is scary at first, but can lead to great success as well as great personal satisfaction.

While this book covers a number of topics, it serves as an introduction to so many areas. As you read through the chapters you will inevitably find areas of interest in which you will want to seek out additional books. However, by the time you are finished reading, you should have a full overview of what it takes to start as a coach and build a business.

Additionally, as Monroe Mann pointed out in the original version, "While the journey is going to be fulfilling, it is also going to be difficult and challenging, and sometimes it is going to drive you absolutely nuts. But don't fret! This is normal, and is part of the process. All entrepreneurs go through this from time to time."

Having written a number of books for entrepreneurs in various fields, I can certainly agree wholeheartedly that this is the case—starting a business is not easy and takes time and dedication. Starting this particular type of service business also takes dedication to your clients. They will depend on you and you will need to be there for them. It is a field in which your clients come first. It's not all about what you've done or how you do things—it's about guiding them to their own successes. With that in mind, this is not a field in which to "dabble."

So, read this book with an open mind and use it as a guide.

You may decide to train and become a coach, but not run your own business. You may decide to run a business, but to keep it small. Or, you may decide to grow your business as far and wide as possible. There are many possibilities—it's up to you to make them happen!

Prepare to Get Motivated

Congratulations! You've just made a brave step into a field that few people understand, and even fewer can actually do well. Welcome to the wild world of motivational and life coaching.

Why is this such a unique field? Well, first off, a lot of people get the wrong idea about the field; the term *motivational coach* is at best misleading, and at worst, misunderstood and ridiculed. Second, it's a unique field because it's somewhat of a hybrid field; it's not standard consulting where you provide specific business information to someone from a position of expertise, and it's not psychotherapy, where issues of mental health are handled by professionals with licenses and degrees.

Motivational coaching falls in a very strange place somewhere in between consulting and therapy, and to add even more confusion, at one point of the triangle there's this additional word thrown in: "motivational." So it's consulting meets psychotherapy with a motivational twist.

Then there is "life coaching," which is essentially what takes place in-between the high energy moments of motivational coaching. In essence, life coaches help individuals manage that which goes on in daily life by keeping their clients focused, maintaining order, and making sure they have a plan and are sticking to it.

Let's face it, most of the day to day aspects of life aren't dynamic or exciting enough to get pumped up over. Most people's daily routines do not require the need for constant motivation. Someone cheering you on, and motivating you, to read a book for school or to organize the mess in your office will probably wear thin pretty quickly. The life part of coaching is to help you find concrete solutions that will keep you on track. The motivational aspect looks at the bigger picture and motivates you to reach the goal of passing the course or getting work done more quickly. Can you do both? Certainly, you almost have to in order to get results.

The Evolution of the Motivational Coaching Field

As far as I am concerned, Tony Robbins really put motivational coaching on the map. While certainly there are the greats such as Dale Carnegie and Napoleon Hill, it was Tony Robbins who really took motivational coaching to an international level and made it a modern craze.

This concept of motivation expanded into finance with Robert Kiyosaki and the Rich Dad series, Robert Allen, and Suze Orman; into real estate with Carlton Sheets, and Donald Trump and Trump University; into the stock market with Investools and Robert Allen, and the list goes on.

Over the last 25 years, motivation moved from being a fringe industry into the international spotlight, in large part thanks to the internet and the ease of communication that email brought into nearly every home. Motivational coaching is no longer something that "those people" do; it's something that is starting to intrigue even Joe Public in Anytown.

Some People Just Won't Change

This discussion of the growth of motivational coaching leads to an interesting fact: While the number of people who are interested in motivational services these days has greatly increased, the vast majority of those who seek such help don't really change their lives all that much as a result of what they've learned. While I am coaching people today who ten years ago might not have hired me, it is also clear that not everyone I coach soars to new heights. Some just refuse to change. I provide them the information and get them inspired, but they just fizzle out. Sure, many of my clients do take what I give them and run with it to the tops of their field, but others take what I give them, put the information in a closet, and return to their old ways of doing things. While this is disappointing, there is not much I can do about it. And there won't be much you can do about it, either. Some people are scared of change and many are set in their ways. That's what makes us all unique. Therefore, not everyone will benefit from a coach.

You see, statistics show that if 100 people attend a seminar, only 30 of them will actually act on the information provided, even if they agree completely with the actions recommended. Why is this? Well, for one, people are generally lazy, no matter what they may tell you or lead you to believe. Second, most people don't want to actually work to change their life; they want a quick fix that doesn't require hard work. They would really like to see change in their lives, but they don't want to *change themselves* in the meantime to help effect that change in their lives. Unfortunately, the quick fix doesn't exist, and many people just give up. It takes hard work to make a change.

> **⚠ Beware!**
> Do not call yourself a psychotherapist unless you are licensed to do so.

This point is crucial. Just because there has been a large increase in curiosity for motiva-

Stat Fact
Most people who attend seminars do not implement what they learn from seminars. The same is true of those who use coaches for a brief stint, and then stop. This is why it is in your best interest to work with clients over a period of time. The accountability you provide the client over a long-term coaching period will result in better results.

tional coaching and services, it doesn't mean that there is a large change in the psychological tendencies of human beings. Most people still remain unwilling to do what they know they need to do in order to become and remain successful.

All Coaching Needs to Be Motivational

The other key transition is that everyone is starting to demand that all coaching—no matter what the field—needs to be motivational. Today, clients not only want the expert analysis, but they also want to be instilled with the confidence to know that they can implement the new plan. They want the passion to come with the plan. They want to be inspired to take the leaps of faith that they just couldn't do alone. They want—and crave—the validation that they just can't find anywhere else.

Yes, today, coaching of *any* sort needs to be motivational, and most consultants will agree that their approach today is beginning to morph to include aspects of coaching, and motivational coaching at that. Isn't it rather funny, though, that it is even called *motivational* coaching—as if there are other branches of coaching that are not motivational? How can anyone be a good coach without being motivational? It seems so obvious. Whether you are coaching a basketball team or a five-person computer programming group; the cast of a feature film or an individual entrepreneur; the CEO of a company or a police officer on the local force; it's all the same—if you're not motivational, you are not doing your job! If you are not helping them to realize that the plan is doable, and is going to be successful, what kind of coach are you anyway? And it all involves the magic five-syllable word: Mo-ti-va-tion-al.

Tip...

Smart Tip
Read this book with a "no rules" frame of mind. What works for you may differ from what I recommend here. Every company is unique, and needs to be approached as such. Don't be afraid to break the rules.

You Need to Be Motivated Before All Others

Surprise! In order to be a motivational coach, you need to first be a motivated *person*!

What does that mean? It means that you can't just *say* that you're a motivational coach; you need to embody it, and mean it. To that end, it's nothing more than having a passion for igniting and fueling a fire within someone else, especially when they think that they can't do it.

The key to take away from this introductory section is that *you need to be an exciting person!* Sure, it seems like an obvious necessity that you need to be motivated first, but a lot of people don't get that. They think that just because they understand the subject matter they are coaching—voila—they are going to have a successful coaching business. WRONG.

You need to be that "first mover" that Aristotle talks about; that force that inspires motion in others. You need to be the inspiration for your clients. If they don't see the fire within you from the moment the relationship begins, you are never going to be able to ignite it within them.

Life Is Still Going to Suck Sometimes

Want the harsh reality? Being a motivational coach to others is perhaps one of the most difficult jobs in the world, and for one reason: It is sometimes incredibly hard to motivate others when you yourself are not.

You see, just because you are motivational and inspiring to others does not mean that you are impervious to depression, loneliness, doubt, fear, and self-consciousness yourself. In fact, you, as a motivational coach, may in fact be more in tune with these psychological issues within yourself than any of your clients.

The point here is that being a motivational coach is not always fun. Some days, you are going to look at your appointment book, and think, "Helping someone else out today is really the last thing I want to do right now." Some days—it is inevitable—you are going to receive some bad news about some aspect of your *own* career or life. Many times, this bad news will arrive right before a scheduled meeting with a client. That is going to bring you down, and you are not going to want to be a motivational coach anymore. In fact, at times like this, you may question whether you are even qualified to be a motivational coach. You'll start thinking, "Maybe I'm just a charlatan!"

There is some good news here: Don't worry about it! All this means is that you are human, and that just as your clients aren't superhuman, neither are you.

My clients ask me constantly, "But who is *your* coach?" True, I myself do have my own coaches and mentors, from Jay Conrad Levinson to my various professors at grad school. But they aren't the ones who get me motivated on a daily basis. Who is then? The answer is clear. My clients! It is by helping my own clients, and seeing their eyes light up, and seeing their hopes and dreams come alive within their own souls that gets me pumped up again about my *own* hopes and dreams.

The end result is that—without fail—I always feel like a million bucks after a client meeting, no matter how depressed I felt going into the meeting. That's one of the best lessons I can give you: As a motivational coach, you need to force yourself to go meet with a client even if you don't feel like it. Once you do, you'll be glad you did. As they say in showbiz, the show must go on!

> **Tip...**
>
> **Smart Tip**
>
> There's a strange phenomenon that you will encounter over and over again: When you are depressed and don't want to meet with a client, the best thing you can actually do is go ahead with the client meeting anyway. Why is this? Simple: Your clients are going to end up motivating you!

> **Beware!**
>
> You too are going to become depressed sometimes. This is okay, as long as you understand from the outset that you are an entrepreneur first, and a motivational coach second. All entrepreneurs feel down sometimes. Just because you become a motivational coach doesn't mean you are incapable of feeling sadness and defeat. Do not think of yourself as a failure if you yourself become depressed along the way. It's all to be expected.

Create Your Own Accountability

Another nice byproduct of being a motivational coach is that all of your clients, and all of the people on your email list (a list which you are soon going to start amassing), are going to start to depend on you as a beacon of light and inspiration. From day one, their hopes and dreams are going to start falling on your shoulders—and you are going to start to feel obligated to these people.

Why is this good? Well, at that point, you are less likely to give up. The more people who find their hope and inspiration in *you*, the less likely you are going to have the guts to abandon what you started when the going gets tough.

Just knowing that others might give up if I do is enough to get me thinking—do I really want to be responsible for others giving up their dreams? No matter how bad things ever get at my end, I can never give up, because if I did, I would be encouraging others to do so—and that is simply not acceptable.

Smart Tip

Tip...

Despite your accomplishments, you want others to relate to you, feel that they know you, and to feel that they too can be successful. To that end, let people know that you too have struggled or are struggling, and show them how you—the motivational coach—are getting through it.

Wrap Up

If you want to successfully motivate others, you need to be motivated yourself. In this field people will rely upon you to get behind them and help them reach their goals. Sure, you will have your own bad days, but you must plow through. You owe it to your clients. Even if you only have one client who is making strides, you owe it to him, or her.

Clearly not everyone is going to respond to your coaching methods or to you as an individual. This is a very personality driven field, so don't be upset if you do not "click" with every client. And even when you do "click" with someone, don't be discouraged if they do not follow-through and make a change.

As for getting started in this business, like any business, you can't just jump in cold, hang out a sign and be a motivational coach. You need to have some credibility. Singers know how to sing, dancers are trained to dance and chefs know how to cook. Would you open a restaurant with someone who had no cooking experience? Of course not. With that in mind, you need to read books about motivational coaching, watch webinars, go to seminars and take classes. You can study specific fields and gain expertise, but you don't have to be the best at something to coach others to excel. You just need to learn all about it. There are many baseball coaches who are not as good as the players they coach. The key is, they know the techniques thoroughly. They know exactly how you are supposed to swing the bat or throw a certain pitch. Your job is to know what it takes to motivate people in general. What gets their hearts pumping faster? What gets them visualizing their success? What makes them truly believe that they can accomplish their goals?

Start doing your homework and lots of it. When you feel that you are trained and ready to motivate people, then just get out there and do it.

What Is a Motivational Coach?

While there are indeed similarities between coaching and consulting, there is also a distinct difference between the two, and in fact, another big difference between coaching and *motivational* coaching.

Consulting is primarily focused on information. You go to a consultant when you know what you want to accomplish, and just need an expert to tell you what needs to be done. Coaching, on the other hand, takes consulting to a higher level. Not only must you be that expert that your clients seek, but now you must also guide them and tell them what you think they should do. A consultant can provide important data, but a coach provides the added benefit of opinionated information reflecting his or her experience and expert analysis—actually telling the client what should be done.

Taken a step further, *motivational* coaching now adds some inspiration to the mix, with the intent of inciting action and forward motion. Now, instead of just being a batting coach on the sidelines passively watching the game play out, you are now out on the field, screaming motivation, pushing for progress, and demanding nothing less than success.

The Differences Between Consulting and Motivational Coaching

Think of it this way:

1. A consultant is someone who tells you what books you need to read in order to get the job done.
2. A coach is someone who then takes that material from the books and explains how it applies directly to your particular situation.
3. A motivational coach then is someone who then grabs you by the shoulders, turns you towards your goals, and then starts pushing you forward, one step at a time, continually pushing, continually refining, continually inspiring, and continually developing while reading from the very books cited before.

In other words, when you choose to become a motivational coach, you are taking on a big burden. You not only have to know what you're talking about (consultant) and know how to apply it to someone else's life (coach), but you now also need to know how to encourage someone else to take action on the wonderful information you are providing, and provide the essential accountability we all need in order to move forward in life (motivational coach).

Misconceptions about Motivational

Here's a big red warning flag! The idea of being a motivat[ional] motivational speaker often has a bad reputation. We see the id[ea] used as the butt of countless numbers of jokes. Do I think this is [?] do! However, more than that, I have found it all helpful.

I see too many up-and-coming so-called motivational coaches [?] performance rather than substance. The way they dress, the way they talk, the way they write; everything about them is overkill to the point of absurdity, goofiness, and with many, downright insincerity.

Do not *act* like a motivational coach—just become one! Truly, you don't need to necessarily do anything differently. Just know your stuff, know how to apply it to others, and know how to inspire others to action.

It's that last part (knowing how to inspire others to action) where a lot of people stumble. Remember, just because you're the expert, and just because you know how to fix other people's problems, doesn't mean you know how to *inspire* them to fix their problems. In other words, just because you're a success doesn't mean you know how to teach that success. Remember that, always.

The Overabundance of Consultants

Consulting is a lot easier than coaching. This is why I believe you run into more consultants than coaches: coaching is harder! You are required to be more, do more, and know more.

- A consultant doesn't need to have a winning personality. A coach most certainly does.

- A consultant can get away without charisma. A coach needs it in droves.

- A consultant provides information but takes no responsibility for what happens with it; a coach, on the other hand, is expected to drive that information into action and make sure the client follows through.

It should be clear to you now that a coach has a lot more to do than a consultant. That's great if you understand that. Just don't fall into the trap of acting motivational in an effort to be more than a consultant. That projects a falseness that is a turn-off to prospective clients, so try to avoid that.

More Than Just Motivation

Folks, don't think that all you need to do is to say, "Rah rah, come on, you can do it" to your clients and you'll become a world-class motivational coach. You are not just a cheerleader. I know a lot of people who make me feel good, but I would never pay a single dime to any of them to guide me with my life. Motivational coaching is more than just initial inspiration; it involves a lot of hard work, commitment, and follow through.

Become Known as the Motivational Expert

In addition to being motivated, your clients need to be inspired by you too. This is where being known as the expert comes in handy. This is also where the fact that you know how to apply that expertise to their career comes in handy too. A motivational coach is someone who is a true part of the team, coaching from the field, with a real vested interest in a successful outcome. One of the biggest reasons my clients give me repeat business is because they say, "He not only talks the talk, but he also walks the walk." In other words, I am not just some critic on the side; I am also in the arena. I am not just giving blind advice, but instead, am also doing for my own career exactly what I am urging my clients to do for theirs. As I tell them they need to write out the table of contents of a book, I am finishing up the table of contents on one of mine. When I encourage a client to put together a budget for a film they want to produce, they know that I am actively producing feature films of my own. There is a feeling of trust my clients have when working with me because they know I am not giving them advice based on what I read about in a book; instead, I am giving them advice based on what I have learned from my own successful experiences.

In other words, you need to do more than just motivate with talk; you also need to inspire your clients with your own acts and deeds.

Be a Role Model

Along with being a motivational coach, I produce films, write books, pursue my graduate degrees, and so forth. It's not specifically about what activities I do that makes

Beware!
Note that I am not saying that you need to have succeeded at the highest level with you own various projects before starting your motivational coaching firm (I certainly did not); all I am saying is that you can be very effective if you are currently pushing for the very same goals and dreams that your clients have. They will be more forthcoming with you, and they are more likely to want to become your client, if you do.

me a role model as a motivational coach, nor how successful the end product turns out to be. The point is that I am motivated to fulfill my goals and dreams. Since my emphasis is on the arts, I have greater success as a role model to individuals in the arts. And yet I can still motivate someone who is trying to write grants for a business or start their own business. A motivational coach motivates by getting out there and doing things. You need to walk the walk and share your stories with your clients or your audience if you are a speaker. As long as you are actively improving upon what you do, you can serve as a role model for those who are not taking any forward steps.

Keep Growing and Never Stop Learning

The only way you are going to keep your current clients is by ensuring that you are growing right alongside them. If you help your clients succeed, but are not adding additional experience and expertise to your name along the way, you risk eventually losing your clients to someone else, who is more experienced and might have more education and more clout. Remember, you are not just motivating someone. That is a given. To become and remain competitive, you have to go beyond the motivation, and be sure you are constantly adding more and more credentials to your name.

You Can't Make Someone Change

There is a huge misconception among many up-and-coming motivational coaches. They somehow believe that it is their job to get their clients to do something. Indirectly, yes, that is the mission, but it's more complicated than that.

Tip...

Smart Tip
You need to make cogent arguments to your clients in such a way that they understand how important the prescribed action is to take, and can decide for themselves that it is the right decision to make.

You see, there is only one person who can make someone do something— and that is the other person. You can't make someone do something. No matter how important you may know a task to be for a client, if the client himself doesn't see the need or the benefit in doing it, then he won't do it.

Therefore, part of the art of being a motivational coach is inspiring trust in YOU. Your negotiation skills need to be top-notch as a

Smart Tip

Remember, only one person can change your client's life—your client. Each client needs to take ultimate responsibility for his life and career. In the end, there is only so much that a coach can do for them.

motivational coach, not only to get them as a client, but to get them to do what you know they need to do.

Often, clients will come to you with a preconceived notion of what they need to do for their own career and life, and only want reassurance. Yet, often you may know from experience that there is in fact an even better way. You can't just tell them; you often have to nudge them into your way of thinking through diplomacy.

Too many motivational coaches try get people excited and pumped up, and then just tell their client what to do, expecting that the clients will blindly follow. However, very few people are going to blindly follow you. And that's actually a good thing; we all want to feel in control of our own lives, and feel that we are making the decisions— not because someone told us to—but rather, because making the decision is in the best interest of our future.

Choose Your Clients Wisely

Along these same lines, when you are pre-interviewing clients to see if you and the potential client will be a good match, one of the key things you need to look for is whether this person is someone who follows through. If you have a client who says they are going to do things but never does, that's not good. It's not good because it is indescribably draining on you. It is incredibly frustrating to have to talk about the same tasks and issues with a client at every single meeting because the client isn't doing what he says he would do.

As you might see, the client relationship has to cut both ways. Your sanity has to come first, not your bank account. Do not welcome clients on board who aren't ready and willing to work; who are just paying you the money because the idea of having a coach makes them feel better. That is meaningless if their lack of action in between meetings makes you feel *worse*! These people need a therapist or a psychologist, perhaps, but not a motivational coach.

This is why during every pre-screening interview, I make it clear that I have no interest in hard selling them into closing the deal. I tell them up front that some people work really well with me, and others do not. I make it clear that if they decide to work with me, they have to really be willing to work and to work *hard*. They will need to do the homework, do the research between meetings, and to actually put into action all of the great plans we assemble. Now *that* is what excites me! Nothing gets me more pumped up than to speak to a client and hear in the first 30 seconds how much they accomplished, and how far they have come since the last meeting. That is just plain exciting! That gets *my* adrenaline pumping. And that is what makes coaching worthwhile—when you hear the excitement in your client's voices, and see it in your client's eyes; when you know that they too are excited because of how much they accomplished. When clients make it unequivocally clear that you have helped them succeed, that feeling is simply priceless.

How to Coach

Coaching at its core is rather simple. You do the following:

- ask probing questions to get to the heart of the matter
- listen to what the clients have to say
- empathize with their situation, and
- guide them firmly forward.

In a typical one-hour session, I start off with a minute or two of pleasantries, then get down to business by asking, "Okay, so what have you been up to?" I work through the hour by asking my clients questions about their projects, their finances, their marketing, etc., and listening to what they have to say in response. I listen intently to their tone of voice and how they are saying things, and if in person, I watch their body language.

Given my years of doing this, I can now usually tell if someone is hiding something, not being completely honest, or is hinting at something else entirely just by their tone of voice or their body language—and that's a key skill you are going to soon pick up. When I notice something that I think a client needs to discuss, I will stay on that issue longer until it feels like we should move on. On the flip side, I am very cognizant of time, and will sometimes deliberately change the subject just so that we cover a variety of topics during each meeting.

The entire time, I am giving my clients homework. If I realize that a client should do something during the week, I always say, "Okay, write that down. Add that to your to-do list." By the end of the hour, the client always has a brand-new, focused to-do list based on what we discussed.

Review Everything

At the end of the session (which I allow to run over time if necessary), we then go over everything we discussed during the meeting for a few minutes. I ask my clients if they have any questions regarding anything we didn't cover. I also go over my own checklist of housekeeping items to ensure that the client has homework from all avenues for the next week. For me, the checklist includes such items as:

- attitude and psychology
- projects and book ideas
- finances and investing
- marketing and sales
- long-term strategy

This list helps me to ensure that I am not forgetting any major instructional areas. At the end of every meeting, I look over this briefly and verify that I covered everything that needed attention during that meeting. Usually, even if we didn't cover every area, I will still ask for a quick update on each area, and give some homework items from each area so that each meeting is still comprehensive. And of course, I have a folder for each client, and keep track of how many meetings we've had, what we've been discussing, and what the goals will be for the next meeting. This is crucial.

Create a Flexible Format

The key to successfully coaching someone is to work flexibly around a standard format that you have created. In other words, you should have a coaching playbook that you have as a backup in case you are ever at a loss for what to discuss—the whole idea is that you, as a coach, should never be at a loss for something to say or recommend to your client. This is absolutely key. You are being paid big bucks to be the opposite of quiet. And your playbook will help.

Flexibility is also key. You should allow each call to play itself out based on the client's unique requirements. Some come to me with a single-minded purpose of producing a film, or writing a book, or getting their finances in order, or creating a new marketing strategy. While I will agree with them and start there, I only use that as the jumping off part, and eventually start bringing additional elements into the coaching mix, i.e., in the end, I ensure that we discuss every aspect of a client's career and life. To do otherwise, in my opinion, is a disservice.

> ### Smart Tip
> Tip...
>
> You can train for years and still not be sure if you're ready to coach others. Therefore, just start right now. Today. With each person you coach, every book you read, and every class you take, you are going to get better and better.

Practice Makes Perfect

Finally, you have to realize that your coaching skills—like any skills—are going to be shaky at first, and are going to improve the more you use them. You are going to inevitably get better and better with time. This is why initially, you might consider coaching for free with some friends—just to get the hang of it. Heck, they may love what you do so much that they become your first clients!

In order to improve your coaching skills, at the end of your sessions you should ask your client, "Is this what you were expecting? Is there anything you think I should be doing differently, or better?" That question alone shows that you care and that you truly value your client's business, because you are taking the time to ask how you can improve. And that says *a lot*. Asking these questions has kept many of my clients coming back again and again—and all because they know that I expect them to tell me if I am doing something wrong.

Wrap Up

In this section I clarified the differences between consulting and coaching. Consultants help you see what needs to be done, motivational coaches get behind you to get it done. I also tried to clear up the misconceptions about motivational speaking. It's not just cheerleading.

It's also important to walk the walk and let your clients know that you are motivated and moving forward in your own endeavors. They need not be the same ones as

▲

your clients but the point is to lead by showing that you are taking action. You can then become a role model as someone who accomplishes what they set out to do. No, you may not hit a home run every time, but you are in the game and your goal is to get them off the bench and into the game as well. And finally, no, you cannot make someone change. The only person who can make someone change is that person. All you can do is utilize that which you have learned about motivational coaching AND lead by example.

In the next section we'll talk more the training necessary to become a motivational coach.

Training to Be a Coach

The basics of coaching are rather simple. Essentially, you need to do the following:

- Learn the tools of coaching

- Develop your own coaching modality and style (select a niche if you choose)

▲

- Market yourself to find clients

- Listen to what clients have to say

- Ask questions to better understand their goals, obstacles and individual life situations

- Determine the best manner in which you can help them

- Use your coaching skills and tools to help them find solutions, then guide them toward those solutions

In a typical one-hour session, I start off with a minute or two of pleasantries, then get down to business by asking, "OK, so what have you been up to?" Since my coaching practice is about succeeding in the arts, I work through the hour by asking my clients questions about their projects, their finances, their marketing, etc., and listening to what they have to say in response. I listen intently to their tone of voice and how they are saying things, and if in person, I watch their body language.

Given my years of doing this, I can now usually tell if someone is hiding something, not being completely honest, or is hinting at something else entirely just by their tone of voice or their body language—and that's a key skill you are going to soon pick up. When I notice something that I think a client needs to discuss, I will stay on that issue longer until it feels like we should move on. On the flip side, I am very cognizant of time, and will sometimes deliberately change the subject just so that we cover a variety of topics during each meeting.

During the entire time, I am giving my clients homework. If I realize that a client should do something during the week, I always say, "OK, write that down. Add that to your to-do list." By the end of the hour, the client always has a brand-new, focused to-do list based on what we discussed. This is based on a "practical" coaching modality that I use to work with my clients. Your coaching modality may differ. Some coaches focus more on the inner needs of the client, others are more holistic and many mix practical and emotional aspects of life into their coaching methods.

Review Everything and Stay on Track

At the end of the session (which I allow to run over time if necessary), we then go over everything we discussed during the meeting for a few minutes. I ask my clients if they have any questions regarding anything we didn't cover. I also go over my own checklist of housekeeping items to ensure that the client has homework from all avenues for the next week.

This list helps me to ensure that I am not forgetting any major areas we need to cover. At the end of every meeting, I look over this briefly and verify that I covered everything that needed attention during that meeting. Often coaching sessions can go off course if you do not make an effort to keep your client focused. You want to try to maintain a focus on coaching and not let a reluctant client steer the conversation off on tangents. That being said, new areas of discussion will sometimes arise during the coaching session that can be valid.

> **Smart Tip** **Tip...**
>
> Establish your own methods of coaching. There is no one size fits all because clients and their needs will be different. There are also a vast number of coaching styles, modalities and tools available. Use the techniques and tools that best fit your client and you as a coach.

I also maintain a folder for each client, and keep track of how many meetings we've had, what we've discussed and what the goals will be for the next meeting. This is crucial.

Create a Flexible Format

The key to successfully coaching someone is to work flexibly around a standard format that you have created. In other words, you should have a coaching playbook that you pull from—the whole idea is that you, as a coach, should never be at a loss for something to say or recommend to your client. Your coaching tools are in your playbook and should help guide you through each session.

You should allow each call to play itself out based on the client's unique requirements. Some people come to me with a very tangible single-minded purpose of producing a film, or writing a book, or getting their finances in order, or creating a new marketing strategy. Often working on such practical matters borders on consulting rather than motivational or life coaching. Others clients, however, have issues that run deeper that they need to address before they can move forward. You need to assess where the obstacles lie between their goals and their successes and decide what tools to use and what hat to wear, coach, consultant or whatever you need to be at the moment. Often, you'll be a little bit coach, consultant, psychologist, etc.

Training

The amount of training you will get will vary significantly depending on where you train and how ready you feel to take on the responsibilities of coaching. Some people will simply have more innate ability to connect on an emotional and practical level than others.

David Cantu, who Runs Life Coaching Austin, in Austin Texas, says he was on the higher end of the learning curve with some 2,000 hours of training. Cantu, who now runs life coaching classes, workshops, and Couples Counseling for Success, Hope, and Better Communication, emphasizes the need for training and points out that even some universities today are offering coaching courses. While some coaches focus more closely on practical daily concerns such as the how-to's of funding or executing a specific project, life coaches such as Cantu, work on a broader coaching modality which he defines as; "The process of uncovering and correcting ineffective beliefs about life, and yourself, and applying powerful tools to help create exactly what you want in your life."

If you search on Google for a coaching training course, you'll find plenty of them offering plenty of certifications. Some will promise you great results in a one week or even one day course. Others will be more practical and provide weeks, months or even years of training.

Before you venture into training, you'll want to consider:

- Why you want to be a coach.
- What type of coaching do you want to pursue.
- Whether you want to have a niche or a broader market.

Before you choose a school in which to train, you'll want to ask:

- What is their reputation? (Having many successful coaching graduates is the best answer)
- How many years have they been in business?
- How transparent are they about their curriculum, teachers, costs, etc.? (Online-only businesses are often very vague)
- How long does it take to get a coaching certificate? (Two days might be a little too quick, while three years may be a bit long, and costly)

Before you start looking for a place in which to train, you'll want to consider what you can bring to the table as a coach. Remember, expertise, connections or plenty of credits in another area do not make you a coach. Many talented people cannot explain how they honed their own talent, nor can they bring that talent forward in someone else. Therefore, if you are a great actor, that does not mean you can coach acting unless you can determine what it is that is holding someone else back from becoming a successful actor. This doesn't mean getting them the right headshot photographer or to their auditions on time. It means what is internally holding them back from doing what they need to proceed in their career.

Before you begin training to be a coach you will also want to ask yourself:

- Do I have an innate understanding of common human behaviors?
- Am I able to listen to someone carefully and actually hear what they are really trying to say—not just on the surface?
- Can I connect on an emotional, and not just practical, level with people?

As a coach you are someone who intervenes in an individual's skills and development, so you take on a lot of responsibility and hopefully contribute to their growth.

Certified Training

Letters after your name typically indicate that you have taken the time and effort to educate yourself in any number of possible areas from business to law to nursing. In an effort to have greater credibility and a deeper understanding of coaching, you should get trained and certified in coaching. Since there is no licensing which means that, unlike a lawyer, anyone can technically go out and call themselves a coach. This however can be a disservice to clients and potentially backfire if your client decides to sue you for misrepresenting yourself and ultimately doing more harm than good. Remember, once you take money and promote yourself as someone providing a service, the legalities of what you do start moving into a gray area. And in a litigious society, it's better to be safe than sorry.

But certification is more than just protection from lawsuits. You want to be trained and certified in coaching to actually maximize your ability to help other people. You will be working with clients on solving problems and helping them reach THEIR goals, not yours. Therefore, even if you provide clients with a blueprint of your own road to success (and a good motivational coach should lead by example) do not expect that they, or anyone, will follow the same exact path that you have taken. They won't! Your success is good for overall motivation, but it is far more important that you focus on your client's goals and not on bolstering or boasting about your own credentials. Coaches typically take back seats and enjoy it.

Proper training and certification also sets you apart from the many coaching wannabes who have not taken the time to learn the craft or hone their skills. It gives you a leg up on the competition.

Where to Train

One of the most significant training institutes is the International Coaching Federation (ICF). Founded in 1995, ICF is based in the United States and operates regional service centers in Asia-Pacific, Europe, and Latin America. They have trained over 8,000 coaches worldwide. ICF defines coaching as partnering with clients in a thought-provoking and creative process that inspires them to maximize their personal and professional potential. They offer:

- Associate Certified Coach (ACC) credentials for the coach with at least 100 hours of client coaching experience.
- The Professional Certified Coach (PCC) credential for coaches with at least 750 hours of client coaching experience.
- Master Certified Coach (MCC) credentials for the expert coach with at least 2,500 hours of client coaching experience.

According to David Ellzey, CEO of David Ellzey Companies, LLC and an international lead trainer for the personal growth technique known as The Sedona Method, "There are industry wide standards that make you a respected coach. If you want to make a career or an income at it, and work with processionals, they'll ask if you are certified with ICF." Ellzey, who coaches a wide variety of individuals and is also a speaker and an author, adds that a good coach should have a holistic approach. With that in mind he recommends the Coaches Training Institute, (CTI). "They have really great founders who are very good at helping

Beware!

Not all certification is the same. Anyone can offer certification. Therefore some certification is not worth the paper it is printed on. It is up to you to do some research and find coaching schools and training facilities that have credibility in the industry. Remember, consumers—or clients—are very savvy these days and have the Internet at their fingertips. They can do research and find out all about the place(s) in which you have trained.

maximize people's potential on all levels including the spiritual, physical and material realm of success. I highly recommend them for those reasons," adds Ellzey

CTI boasts over 35,000 trained coaches worldwide with a program lasting roughly one year followed by a six month virtual certificating program. Their specially designed program teaches the Fundamentals, Fulfillment, Balance, Process and Synergy leading up to certification.

Also recommended, among the many coaching modalities is the Results Coaching System, originally from Australia, from which 6,000 coaches have been trained worldwide. Another successful program is Neuro Linguistics Programming (NLP), which dates back to the1970s and has been used by Tony Robbins. NLP also offers certification.

Any one of these coaching modalities (or a combination of a couple) can provide you with the training and certification you will need to get started as a professional coach.

Tools of the Trade

Every profession has some tools of the trade, whether it's a dentist's drill, psychologist's personality tests or a lawyer's briefs. In your case, as a coach, your tools are usually intangibles that you learn in order to facilitate the best results from your clients. Of course your tools will vary depending on where you are trained. In recent decades, a lot of time and effort has been spent on the study of the most effective means of starting coaching conversations, assessing information and establishing a system that works for both coaches and clients.

You will likely find that from courses en route to certification, coupled with your own selected reading, you will inevitably end up with coaching tools based on what you've learned coupled with your own theories, personality and life experiences. In the end you want your Coaching practice to be, as David Ellzey describes it, "a modality that helps people shine."

Your tools, which are verbal and/or written, may vary, depending on where you study but they should help you:

- Recognize and/or uncover the goals that are unique and inspiring to each client. These can be are short, medium and long term goals. It's important to remember: Without goals what is there to even be motivated about?

▶

'our clients with setting their own
It is important that they are not
g after goals that are set for them
ir families, schools, society or even
you!

> **Smart Tip** Tip...
>
> Learn how to guide a
> conversation so that
> your clients come up with
> their own great ideas that you
> can support. Bringing out
> their best is part of your job.

- Understand the best manner in which your client takes in, absorbs and codes information in the brain.

- Help clients replace excuses with solutions.

- Teach your clients about positive self talk, which is a powerful tool that can be utilized in all aspects of life to reinforce self esteem and performance.

- Listen carefully so you can hear the subtle commentary that's underneath the words your client is saying. This will help you reach a deeper level.

- Assess what it is that is blocking your client from moving forward…what barriers he or she has set up. For example, you may use an open ended question such as "can you tell me what stands between you and reaching that goal?" This can apply to an executive looking for a promotion or an actor trying to land a role.

- Get your client to move from point A to point B in the most effective manner that meets their needs.

Life Coach and Global NLP trainer, Nicole Schneider, who has been coaching since 1996, compares coaching to preparing a meal. "There are a bunch of ingredients that can be combined in different ways to create a lot of meals. In coaching, there are always multiple ways of getting from point A to point B so you have to explore the options." Schneider, who is based in Florida, Los Angeles and Amsterdam, depending on the time of year, explains that coaching "Is not simply advising people. If you give advice based on your map of the world, you can actually advise people on the wrong stuff. Coaching is really having the capabilities to help people by guiding them to what they want. They come with the answers, the discoveries and the awareness. You streamline and guide them by removing the obstacles."

Know Your Clients

Clients come in all shapes and sizes. It's important that you get to know them and know them well. For this reason it's important not to try to expand your practice too quickly. Your first few clients will provide you with an opportunity to establish a rapport while learning what they are all about. What makes them tick? What is their personality type? For example, are they extroverts or introverts? How do they approach a coaching session? Some people show up ready to jump right in while others will talk about everything but their needs, goals or the real reason for being there. As a good judge of people you will learn how to interact with each client. This is an integral part of successful coaching.

Getting to know your clients typically means taking good notes. No you don't need to know everything about them, but you do want to write down key information as they talk. You'll also want to take some notes on body language and their manner of presenting information. For example, you might write down that he or she is very tense or looking at the floor often while talking to you. This could indicate that someone is ashamed of his or her actions, or lack thereof.

After a session you should give yourself a few minutes to enter notes into an ongoing file on each client. With that in mind, many coaches, not unlike therapists, schedule appointments fifteen minutes apart to write their notes and do their filing. While you may, in time, have a staff, it's important that you read your own notes and handle the filing of your client's data for several reasons. First, this is highly personal information and even the best assistant may discuss it with friends or family members outside of the office. You need to protect client confidentiality. Secondly, reading and writing in a client's files helps you get to know each client and follow their progress. The better you know your clients the more likely they will trust you and want to continue working with you.

All that being said, you may not always be the right fit for a client, especially if you have a specific niche. If a client falls outside of your niche, you should be able to recommend them to another coach or at least point them to a good website for locating coaches. Just as your practice will grow based on client referrals, you may also get referrals from other coaches, as they too may find that they are not the right fit for a certain client. Nicole Schneider points out that some women may want to discuss women's issues and may simply feel more comfortable with a female coach. Likewise, you as a male coach may feel

Smart Tip

While note taking, don't get into the habit of looking at your notepad, laptop or notebook computer. Try to maintain eye-contact as often as possible and glance down when necessary. Remember, spelling doesn't count but a good working rapport does.

Tip...

that you are not the right person with whom to discuss women's issues. In either case you would refer to another coach. As Schneider puts in "When in doubt refer out,"

It is, therefore, advisable to get to know other coaches. While they may be your competition, the reality is that you can also learn from one another and benefit from having some allies in the field.

A Coaching Job

While this book is about starting your own coaching business, you might cut your teeth in the industry by starting out coaching for someone else's business. Just as there are sections later on in this book dedicated to hiring outside coaches if your practice becomes too much for you to handle, other coaches may also be hiring. If you have credentials, especially from one of the leading training centers such as ICF or CTI, you can apply to work as a coach for someone else's business as a way of honing your skills. You'll want to find someone with whom your own training methodology and tools align, at least to some degree. A coaching job may not make you rich, but it's a stepping stone on your way to later opening your own business. And, if you are good, some of your clients may follow you as you embark on your own coaching business venture.

Practice Makes Perfect: Honing Your Coaching Style

Actually, you will never be perfect as a coach—you will keep evolving with each new tool in your repertoire and each new client that you meet.

You can however, improve dramatically as you work with clients. By using various coaching tools, you will see which ones provide your clients with the best results and which ones simply do not work for you. You will also see which style is best suited for your coaching needs. For example, some coaches are more assertive while others motivate in more subtle manners. Some coaches ask a lot of questions while others guide their clients by making suggestions and giving them assignments. Just as there will be some trail and error in running your business and setting your prices, there may be some trail and error in honing your own coaching style. The various modalities of coaching along with your own personality and how you interact with other people will all produce your style of coaching.

Coaching vs. the Business of Coaching

Much of the rest of this book focuses on the business side of coaching, hence the title *Start You Own Coaching Business*. Therefore, it is up to you to train in coaching modalities and to become certified as a coach. You want to have the expertise and confidence as a coach before you hang out a shingle. Since coaching is largely based on word of mouth, you must have a good reputation. Word of mouth can also work against you—people love to post negative comments on the Internet - more than they like to post words of praise.

Successful coaches, such as David Ellzey and Nichole Schneider, know their crafts inside and out. Like professional ice skaters who have been skating from the age of three, coaching is ingrained in who they are. They can talk about coaching at length and as is the case with anyone who wants to be successful in any type of business, they know the industry very well. Once you are very comfortable with your skills and abilities you can focus much more of your attention on growing your business.

It is also once you are comfortable as a coach that you will start to develop your own opinions, ideas and theories about coaching. You may question some techniques while praising others. You may even create your own hybrid coaching technique. It is at this point (when you have something to say) that you can enhance yourself as a coach as well as your new (or upcoming) business by writing blogs and articles for your own web site and for other sites. While maintaining the privacy of your clients, you may illustrate what you have done successfully to help them succeed.

In time, you may even gather enough material or have enough of your own theories or experiences to write a book. Most coaches wait until the time is right to write a book. Reputation is so important in coaching and you do not want to have a book that does not illustrate who you are or offer something worthwhile. You'll want to build your reputation on solid ground based on what you have learned and can offer the book buying audience about coaching.

As your business grows, so will your business needs. This is when you will need to be very careful to keep both plates spinning at one time. Remember, you cannot neglect your coaching skills or your focus on your clients. Psychologists, dentists, lawyers and other professional service providers have, on occasion, become so immersed in their business needs

> **Tip...**
>
> **Smart Tip**
>
> Create a schedule for yourself that provides you with time for honing your coaching skills and also for running your coaching business.

29

that they forget about doing what is best for the patients or clients. This has not turned out well. In short, don't let that happen to you. Separate your coaching from your coaching business and work hard to keep both running smoothly.

Wrap Up

In this section, coaching training is discussed and the importance of being prepared to take on a coaching career and start your own business. Listed are several leading places in which you can train and become certified as a coach—this enhances your credibility significantly. It's also of great importance that you understand the tools of the trade.

The chapter also touched upon the idea of knowing your clients well and the importance of taking notes during sessions and maintaining your files as you go. The better you know your clients the more likely they will feel comfortable working with you…and that means they will stick around. There was also some talk about coaching skills versus the business of coaching. One is a trained skill and the other is having business knowledge. They are different. It is not unlike a chef who knows how to cook but does not know how to run a restaurant or a contractor who can fix anything, but cannot manage his or her business in order to make a profit. You wear two hats once you start a coaching business and that is "coach" and "business owner"

It is also important that you stay up to date on what is going on in the coaching industry and align yourself with other coaches. Sure some will be your competition, but many coaches will help one another with referrals and other mutual benefits.

The most important aspect of this chapter is to learn and train before you hang a coaching shingle outside of your door. Credibility is important and you need to be that much more proficient and knowledgeable in the coaching field than your clients.

First Steps
Setting Up
Your Business

When you first start thinking about setting up in your business, one thing to consider at length is the name of your company. One difficulty startup entrepreneurs sometimes have when making this decision is whether to use their actual name in the name of the company, or to come up with a name that is all its own.

In deciding what to do for your own company, you first have to ask if your name itself means anything; i.e., is your name bankable? Do people associate your name with whatever service you are providing? Are you coming from a field where everyone already knows and respects your name? If so, perhaps you might want to include your name in the company name.

On the other hand, if your name is not associated with success in your industry, you might be better served when starting out by coming up with a creative name that says a little bit about what your company does, like I did with Unstoppable Artists, for instance.

The nice thing about coming up with a company name that doesn't include your own name is that it provides some separation and some privacy. If down the line your name becomes synonymous with whatever type of coaching you are doing, you can always put your name in front of the company; i.e., Monroe Mann's Unstoppable Artists.

Think Big and International

When naming your company—as in everything you do from this point forward— think big! Think international! Realize that your small-town idea could very well soon become a world-wide phenomenon if you want it to be.

To that end, you want to make sure that the name you give your company is a big enough name, and one that will ideally not require any changes as your company grows. In fact, it may be better to choose a name that requires that you grow into it, rather than a name that you quickly grow out of.

For instance, don't use the name of your street in the company name unless that is part of your strategy (example: 57 Piney Lane & Co. vs. Wall Street Insight, Inc.).

Forward Thinking

Try to determine whether your name would make sense in other countries. Is it easy to pronounce? Is there any possibility that it sounds like an offensive word in a foreign language? While to many this may seem like putting the cart before the horse, I truly believe that those people who succeed at the highest level are those who thought far enough beyond the possible so that they were prepared for the impossible. This way of forward thinking has paid off big dividends for hundreds and hundreds of entrepreneurs over the years, and there is no reason to think this strategy won't work for you too.

So think big! Does the name of your company help you give off the reputation you desire? Are you comfortable with the name? Do you feel good about it? Are you excited when you see it, read it, say it, think about it? Does the name make you proud to be associated with it? The answers to all of these questions absolutely must be a loud and reverberating *yes!*

URL Out of Luck

Another consideration when choosing the name of your company is what web URLs are available using permutations of that name. Years ago, entrepreneurs did not have to worry about URLs, but today, if you choose a company name without first checking to see if a logical and corresponding website is available to match, you may be shooting yourself in the foot.

Smart Tip

Tip...

When selecting a name, you have many options. You can become known by including your name in the company name or you can be more generic. Since coaching is a personalized field, having your name can be inviting since you are a professional and people will see you as one. However, the other school of thought is that coaching is not all about you, but about your clients, so you might choose a name that gives them an incentive to move forward.

Does the website URL need to match perfectly? Ideally, perhaps it should, but it is not an absolute requirement. What is required is that the URL is logical, easy to spell, and easy to remember.

For instance, I recently co-wrote a book with Jay Conrad Levinson called *Guerrilla Networking*. The title was not one that could be easily changed, and all of the obvious web domains were taken, including all permutations of GuerrillaNetworking. I tried to think of what other website name I could come up with that might correspond logically to that title. After looking over the concept of the book again (becoming the type of person that other people want to meet), it hit me like a bolt of lightning: www.StopMeetingPeople.com. Easy to remember and easy to spell, it makes sense and it works for this company, which in this case is a book.

The point I am making is that when choosing a name these days, you have to think of more variables than just the name itself. You also have to determine if there is a corresponding web domain to match that will *help* sales, and not hurt them.

Once you find a web domain that you're happy with, your next step is to reserve every possible permutation of that. For example, when I bought Monroe

Mann.com, I didn't just stop there; I bought MonroeMann.net, .biz, and .tv. Then, I logged in to each domain and *forwarded* each one to MonroeMann.com. Now, no matter which domain you type in, you will always end up at MonroeMann.com. Cool, huh?

> ### Smart Tip
> Other URL permutations can be common misspellings and related searches. You'd be surprised how many people end up at your site that way.

Business Formalities

Finally, a quick discussion about the legal formation of your company. If you're a one-person operation, you could legally just open up shop. You don't need to get any legal paperwork, and you could simply use your personal checking account to handle transactions. However, all checks would have to be made out in your name, which may seem less professional to your clients, and mixing personal and business accounting will result in difficulties at tax time.

The next level would be to legally become a sole proprietor by setting up a DBA (doing business as) with your state, county, or city clerk's office (depending on the state you live in). A key consideration is to research the availability of your chosen business name because if the name you want is already taken in your area, then you can't use it. If the name *is* available, it typically costs less than $100 to register, and you'll receive legal formation papers with your company name on it.

With those papers, you can then open a bank account in that name, and also open up merchant accounts at various companies such as PayPal. Becoming a DBA creates a much higher level of professionalism for your company. Instead of having clients write checks out to you personally, they write them out to your company name. These checks are deposited into your business bank account, which will help you tremendously from an accounting standpoint as now business and personal accounts are separate.

Registering your business name also protects you from others using that name. If you are planning for the long term, as you should, you'll want to establish a business identity through a unique, registered name and even possibly a trademarked tagline or logo.

Incorporating and Partnerships

Next, you might consider an LLC, otherwise known as a limited liability company. The benefits of operating as an LLC are that you receive the liability protection of a corporation, but the pass-through tax benefits of a proprietorship. In other words, if someone sues your LLC, your personal assets cannot be seized (which is not the case with a sole proprietorship). Also, instead of having to prepare a separate tax return for the company as a corporation would, an LLC's taxes are actually reported on the tax return of the business owner. The only downside is that it costs more than a DBA to set up an LLC—about $500 to $1000—and it requires a little bit more complicated paperwork during the year. An LLC can be set up very easily at bizfilings.com, incorporate.com, or legalzoom.com.

> **Smart Tip**
>
> *Tip...*
>
> If you're unsure which business formation is right for you, just start out as a sole proprietorship. It's really easy, and you can always upgrade later.

If you bring on additional coaches, you might consider becoming an LLP, or a limited liability partnership. This is very similar to an LLC, except each partner is responsible for his own legal mistakes; i.e., one partner's malpractice will not cross over to the other partners in the firm.

Finally, there are the infamous C and S corporations. Since S corporations are not recognized in many places, and since C corporations are inherently more complicated, I don't recommend either for a startup formation in the field of coaching. While there may be reasons to justify such a formation down the line, when starting out, it is not worth the expense, double-taxation headaches, or paperwork required to use this type of entity.

If you're wondering the path my own company took, I started out from day one as a registered DBA called Unstoppable Actors, and upon my return from Iraq, I turned the company into an LLC, this time called Unstoppable Artists. As my business grows, I am considering the possibility of becoming an LLP to provide liability protection for partners as they are added.

Wrap Up

Naming your company and setting up your business are big events. But don't let them become so big of an event that they prevent you from moving forward. Remember that preparation is just a precursor to the main event. Don't lose momentum because you're so busy preparing! Most importantly, just remember that you can always change the name of your company, and your business will naturally evolve from one form to the next as it grows.

Choosing a
Target Market

No matter where you choose to start your business, you're inevitably going to start having dreams of what it would be like if your business were located elsewhere. To that end, the best place to start your coaching business... is probably right where you are.

In fact, thanks to the ability to use the internet and telephone for coaching, starting your coaching business right where you are makes even more sense than ever before, because the costs are so low. Don't make the mistake of thinking that you have to move to Hawaii because you are helping people with their surfing careers, or to London because you are helping to launch the next UK pop star. Stay where you are! At least for now. Because no matter where you go, you're gonna wish you were somewhere else.

One example I can use to explain this is show business. There are many people who are not doing so well as actors in New York, and they decide that they are going to move to Los Angeles because that is where all the film auditions are. What these people don't realize is that while there may be more film auditions out in L.A., there are also more actors, meaning more competition, meaning whatever problems they were having in New York are just going to multiply when they head for Los Angeles.

Sure, there may be situations where you should open up shop in one particular area only. But if you are just starting out in the field of coaching, you are probably much better off working right in your own area. This way you can learn the ropes, and then down the line, you can take those invaluable entrepreneurial and coaching skills to another locale if you so choose.

Another reason I recommend you start your business right where you are is that any move to another city is inevitably going to slow you down by at least two to three months, if not longer. Why go backwards when you can go forwards—and quickly—right where you are?

Your Target Market

While a niche market such as mine is okay and can be very profitable, your market can also be very broad. Good motivational coaches can work with a wide range of people who fall into the category of "needing direction" or "trying to overcome boundaries" in life.

If you do choose to define your niche market, it may be easier for you to find clients. This is because the more specific you get, the easier it becomes for prospective clients to realize that you can guide them to solutions to their particular problem. Rather than wondering if you know enough about their specific issues, prospective clients will think, "Hey, this coach was made just for me!"

Smart Tip

Tip...

Yes, you can be an effective coach in a niche market if you have experience in that market, but you can also have a wide range of clients. You do not have to have been abused to help people who were or have had a drug problem to coach people who are recovering from such a problem. That's why you need to have the skills and techniques germane to successful coaching.

The World Is Your Oyster

Remember too, that your target market is not just the people in your town. First, if you're good and word gets around, clients will travel to work with you. Second, thanks to the internet and the phone, geography is not an issue. This is another reason why you shouldn't be too broad in the type of client you service—just because there aren't enough people in your own town to support you doesn't mean that there aren't enough people worldwide to in fact do so.

I have clients all over the world, from Europe to South America. Most of these clients I have never met face to face. I work with them by phone, email, and by post, and it works splendidly. But I wouldn't have these clients if I didn't actively mention on my website that it doesn't matter where you live, and that I can help you no matter where you call home.

In addition, no matter how specific you get at the outset with your target market, you can always expand down the line. While I started out focusing only on actors, my client base grew to include artists in general, and now I have found myself expanding to include all entrepreneurs—whether they are in the arts or not. That's the nice thing about starting small and specific: You can always branch out if your original niche proves too small. However, the opposite may not be true.

Keep in mind that it's a mistake to cater to too large a swathe of clients at first. You (and your potential clients) may get confused and overwhelmed. It's best to start with a niche, and grow from there. Otherwise you risk never getting off the ground in the first place.

Being Unique

When it comes to choosing a target market, this is your number one task: Be unique. When it comes to choosing a target market, this is your number one goal: Be one of a kind. Here's the thing: Chances are, there is at least one other company doing a similar type of coaching. I didn't say *the same* type of coaching; just similar. Similar

Beware!
Don't be different just for the sake of it. It's okay to be different if it fits your coaching modality.

idea, similar client base, similar business model—whatever. The key to success then is to make sure that you differentiate yourself from all of that competition, even before you open up shop.

Why Am I Different?

Ask yourself, "Why am I different?" Why is your company different? Why are you yourself different? Why is your company different from every other one out there doing something similar? The more reasons you can provide, the more successful you are probably going to be.

In fact, the more unique your position up front, the easier it is going to be for you to choose your target market as well. When you think about it, that makes perfect sense. The more specific you make your company, the easier it will be for you to find your customers and for your customers to find you too.

The Competition Question

One of the big reasons why a lot of entrepreneurial firms never got off the ground is that they didn't differentiate themselves enough from the competition. If you offer nothing better than the current market leader, then it's absurd to think you are somehow going to pull business away from them. Why would a customer do that? It doesn't make any sense.

You see, prospective clients can do one of two things with their money: They can either spend it with you, or spend it elsewhere. That is why even if you have no direct competition, you are still competing for your client's business. If you are charging $750 for a five-week program in an area where you are the only motivational coach, you are still in competition for that money. All you have to do is ask yourself where else that money could be spent. Think about it. That $750 could be spent on a variety of expenses; groceries, school supplies for the kids, a mortgage or car payment, a credit card bill. The list is truly endless.

And when you look at your competition that way, you come to realize how special you really need to be—not only to make a profit, but to just break even. And this is why you absolutely *must* spend the time wracking your brain to come up with a solid marketing angle; a solid reason why you have something that makes you unique; a solid encouragement for prospective clients to think, "Hey, I could spend my money elsewhere, but investing my money with this motivational coach is going to bring back a better return."

That is how you are going to get clients: by helping them to determine on their own that you are a better investment than anything else. If you do that, you become successful. If you do not do that, you struggle like the vast majority of entrepreneurs worldwide.

Wrap Up

This chapter is one of the most important, because it discusses marketing. Without good marketing, your business is going to sink. And good marketing too is a key part of your preparation. It is also a part of your business that is going to be developing constantly every single day. While preparing a good marketing campaign is key, I also warn you that finding your perfect marketing angle is a time-consuming pursuit. It may take years to find the perfect marketing angle and target market for your business. Just don't give up and you will find it. And don't wait until you have the perfect marketing angle before you get started—that's just an excuse for procrastination.

6

Setting Up Your Office— Online and Off

Welcome to the next generation! You don't need to have an office anymore. You don't need to rent costly meeting places. You don't even need to get dressed up anymore. Thanks to technology and the modern acceptance of comfortable cafes for client meetings (i.e., Starbucks, Panera, etc.), running a client services business has never been easier.

Speaking from my own experience, I used to run the business end of the company from home, and meet with clients either in parks or cafes, or by phone. And it worked perfectly. In fact, it worked so well that even though I now have a nice office, I still lean toward meeting my clients outside of it. It just seems more comfortable.

Home Business or Business Office

Years ago, I actually had a nice swanky office in New York City. When I was deployed to Iraq with my national guard unit, I broke the lease. On my return, I decided to just run the business from home until I got resettled. Turns out that I didn't want to leave. I soon realized that the expense of renting the office was a waste of money, and having to take the train to the city every morning wasn't all that much fun.

By running the office end of my coaching firm from home, I ended up saving $1300 per month in rent. I didn't have to worry about "being at the office" because by virtue of running the business from home, I was always at the office. And to this day when I need to meet clients in person, I meet them in a local café or a place of their choosing. In the warmer months, I meet my in-person clients in a lovely local park. And they all love it! It's hip, it's relaxed, and it's non-presumptuous.

Setting Up Your Office

Perhaps you and your clients seek more privacy. Or perhaps due to the type of coaching you offer, it's more of a hands-on thing; if you are a motivational coach for athletes you can't really do that at Starbucks unless you are discussing business and financial matters. Eventually it may make sense to expand out into an office again.

Nonetheless, when starting out, the point is that you do not need to go overboard in establishing a professional presence. Do not charge up thousands of dollars on your credit cards or drain your bank account when—in my opinion—you don't need to. You need a computer, a website, a cell phone, and a way to handle payments. You may want to also have brochures and business cards. And that's about it.

Your Website

Most importantly, you need a website. These days, if you don't have one, you are considered more than unprofessional; you are considered sketchy. And let me tell you—a sketchy motivational coach doesn't have many clients.

So whether you hire someone else to do it, do it completely yourself, or use a company such as iBuilt.net, it doesn't matter. What does matter is that you take that URL that we discussed earlier and connect it to an actual live website. And don't spend more than $750—even that may be too high.

Your Email List

You need to collect email addresses from those who visit your site. This is really how you help those word-of-mouth referrals to spread. Whether you have an email list of 20, 200, 2000, or 20,000, it is power; it allows you to inexpensively keep your business in the mind of potential customers on a regular basis. You need to make sure you have people's emails by permission and are not sending spam.

By sending out emails to my list with top ten lists, business advice, financial recommendations, audition notices, etc., I help keep my business at the top of subscribers' minds. It also boosts my credibility and expertise.

I also actively encourage my readers to forward the emails I send out on to their friends. The result is that with every email I send out, I end up getting more people to sign up to my email list. It's a beautifully effective process. You just need to make sure the emails you send out have quality content.

Your Phones

Next, you need a phone and/or a cell phone. You don't need to bother getting a separate business phone if you don't want to; certainly not up front. Starting out, I used my cell phone as my primary business phone, and my cell number was the phone number that I included in advertising. If you do decide to move into an office space, you'll probably want separate lines installed at the office. However, when starting out, it just doesn't make any sense to do so. And you'll love not paying the extra phone bill.

Credit Card Processing

You also need a way to process payments. There are literally hundreds of other payment merchant accounts that you can investigate, including one by Google. I use PayPal Pro. Paypal is an e-commerce business allowing payments and money transfers to be made through the internet. It serves as an electronic alternative to traditional paper methods such as checks and money orders. PayPal performs payment processing for users, for which it charges a fee. PayPalPro allows users to take credit card orders by phone. While you will still have the ability to send invoices via email, there is an added professionalism added when you can say, "I can take your card info by phone if you prefer."

If you wish to be acknowledged as a business account, you must link a business checking account to Paypal. And in order to get a business checking account, you must first secure a business license from the state (see Chapter 4).

Brochures and Business Cards

Next, two simple marketing tools: brochures, and business cards. When getting started, you'll want to update your business card and your brochures often, so don't spend a whole lot of money on large quantities that will quickly become outdated.

For the brochure, you can easily buy template paper at an office supply store, and then create the actual brochure in a desktop publishing program. Or save even more money and use blank white paper that you just fold three ways. If you don't have the time or skills for this, then hire someone. Do a Google search, visit Craigslist, or ask around to find freelance design talent for your purposes. If you can't afford to pay try to barter. Another option is looking around for talented students who can get credit in school for the work they do for you.

For your business cards, you can certainly print out your own or use a online company like Vistaprint to set one up for you for free. Some entrepreneurs say that the reason their clients keep coming back is because they save money at every juncture in an effort to keep costs down; apparently, their clients appreciate the gesture. However, you need to be careful about the image you might give off by handing out a poor-quality business card. If it is clear you printed out your business cards yourself (with per-

Smart Tip (Tip...)

Paypal is known around the world as one of the easiest ways for small businesses to accept credit card payments.

forations) or that you got them as a freebie, your credibility will drop greatly.

However, you can get a freelance designer to make a custom card that is well designed and unique, and then find an inexpensive printer online, such as PrintingForLess.com, to get everything printed. My old card was a custom designed folding business card with my photo; my new card is a two-sided card from Vistaprint. These cards not only introduce me and provide important information, but they make a memorable impression on my potential clients. You can also visit well known stores such as Kinkos or Staples.

Putting It All to Work

This is really it—this is about all you need to get started:

- a computer
- internet access
- a website
- a phone
- a way to process credit cards
- brochures
- business cards

Of course, you might be wondering what you should be doing with those brochures and business cards. The business cards are easy; hand them out to everyone and anyone and make sure it says why you are different on the card. For me, it says, "I'm the guy to call when you're ready to take control of your circumstances." That short statement helps to qualify prospects from the business card.

As for the brochure, the idea is to place them in areas that receive high traffic from people who have a need for your services. For my business, I have brochures at various rehearsal studios, bookstores, music shops, etc.

One other tool you might consider is a printed newsletter. While this is more expensive than an e-newsletter, it may be considered a specialty item—because most businesses don't use printed newsletters anymore. Therefore, if you do print a newsletter and send it out to your current clients, it is going to really show you off as someone different and special. While I would not recommend you do this until after you have an established client base, it is something you should be actively thinking about doing down the line in your constant effort to be stand out among your competition.

Dollar Stretcher

Keep your costs low. Anything beyond the list I provided above is a luxury when you're just getting started, and really not necessary. The only way you'll stay in business is to keep your startup expenses as low as you possibly can.

Wrap Up

The most important point in this section is that you do not need a lot of money to set up your office. Look for discounts wherever you can find them and use some creativity to complete the picture.

Your most important needs are a quality computer, a phone and/or cell phone (if you only choose one, get a cell phone, you cannot afford to be unreachable), credit card processing capabilities and some brochures and business cards. You may also add CDs to that list. You also must have a website, one that need not be fancy, but provides the basics on what you do, where you do it (by phone and/or in person) and your range of fees. You should also include where you were trained and your other coaching credentials on your website's About Me page. Remember, your credibility as a coach is your number one selling point. If you just go out and say you are a coach, a lawyer or an astronaut for that matter, you have no credibility whatsoever. One of the fallacies of coaching is that because it does not require a license, anyone can just do it. That is not true.

7

Finding Those
First Clients

Those first clients are right in front of you; at the mall, at the supermarket, at the gas station. Yes, potential clients are everywhere. The key is finding out who they are, and in convincing them that you are someone with whom they should invest their money.

That's how you need to look at what your clients are doing: investing. They are investing in their future. But you can't just tell them that. You need to help them convince themselves of that on their own. They need to come to the conclusion on their own that you are the best, and that you are worth an investment of significant time and money.

So, how do you begin?

First Clients

You have to start by finding those first potential clients. And let me tell you, finding your first clients is either going to be the easiest thing you've ever done in your life, or one of the hardest, and either way, you're screwed. Why?

Well, if the clients come too easy, you're going to think it's always going to be like that and you're dead wrong. And then you're going to get lazy and cavalier, and a few months down the road, wonder why your business is failing.

On the flip side, if the clients come with difficulty, you're going to think it's always going to be like that—and again, you're dead wrong. And then you're going to get discouraged, and want to give up, thinking that it's just not worth the effort.

Don't Quit Your Job

The truth is that you won't know how easy attracting those first clients is going to be until you try. No matter what happens, you have to beware of assuming things are too easy or too hard based on your first forays into the field. Don't let the beginning fool you. To that end, don't quit your day job just because you found your first two clients right out of the starting gate—that's what I did, and I wish I had not. I wish I had kept my regular source of income until I was making enough money part-time from my coaching business to warrant dropping the other job.

You see, shortly after I quit my job, I suddenly realized that those first clients that just fell on my doorstep were flukes, and suddenly, I was struggling in my efforts to get more clients. I desperately wished that I still had my other job. But by then it was too late; I was already in

> **Tip...**
>
> **Smart Tip**
> A lot of people who want and need help do not ask for it. Therefore, pick up the slack and ask them yourself. That's how you get clients.

the "own my own business" mentality, and I couldn't turn back because I was too much entrenched in the entrepreneurial excitement.

Where Are Those First Clients?

So where exactly are these first clients? Chances are, if you've been thinking about becoming a motivational coach in your particular field, you already have some idea about where to look. You probably already know some potential clients.

What if you don't? It could simply mean that it's just time to start asking around. In other words, if what you are offering is great (which it had better be), then it's time to call up all of your friends and ask them for referrals.

Getting the Word Out

Ask for referrals. I know, it sounds scary, crazy, and preposterous. And yet, as we've already discussed, asking people you already know for referrals is perhaps the best and most cost-effective way to gain new clients. In fact, even asking perfect strangers for referrals works wonders as well—and trust me, you'll be doing exactly this once you honestly believe that what you offer beneficial coaching techniques and strategies.

You see, people who are confident in what they have to offer are not afraid to talk about it with anyone they may come in contact with—even perfect strangers—because to do otherwise would be missing an opportunity to potentially help someone. And that is taboo. However, you also do not want to come across as being too pushy or you'll lose their respect.

Other ways to get the word out:

- Put some free ads up on places like Craigslist, or find other free online posting boards where you can put up a free ad.
- Create fliers and brochures and leave them in places where potential clients might find them.
- Write articles and/or blogs for other websites. Look for websites that could use your expertise and contact the site managers or content editors.
- Take out some advertisements in the newspaper.

I include paid advertising as a last resort because I know how costly this can be, especially for a startup company, and I'd hate to see you heavily in debt before the company really even gets a chance to get off the ground. I'll talk about advertising again later, and also include a discussion of Google AdWords, but for now, I really urge you to keep costs as low as possible, and work to get your first clients (and all your clients, in fact) through word-of-mouth referrals and an occasional brochure or flier.

Tell Them You Can Help Them

Lest you think that finding the potential clients is the hardest part—think again. Getting potential clients on the phone or talking is the easy part. The hard part is turning them from potential clients into actual paying clients.

The first key is to let your potential clients know that you can help them. Simple, right? Yet most people don't bother to tell prospective clients how they can do this. Do so! Have some guts and take the plunge.

Sure, the reality is that most of them are going to say "No" in some way. But don't worry about it! The more times you hear "No" the more times you are also going to hear them say, "Yes!" because it really is a numbers game. You just have to keep on asking people for business until some of them inevitably say yes.

You need to have a strong backbone, and be able to withstand rejection after rejection. If this freaks you out, get over it—you're an entrepreneur now, and you have to make those phone calls!

Networking

The only way to get started is to network. Since coaching is a person to person business the best way to let people know that you are offering your services is to look for meetings, conferences and gathering that you can attend. If your coaching is predominantly in the arts, look for theater groups or even a gallery opening. If your audience is primarily business professionals, find out where local business organizations meet even the local Chamber of Commerce. Networking means getting to

Tip...

Smart Tip

Most professionals including lawyers, doctors, psychologists and yes, even coaches don't make cold calls saying "Hi I'm a motivational coach." Get out and network instead and use the web, especially social media to tactfully let people know what you do.

know other people and it is why so many people use LinkedIn and even Facebook. Since it may be hard to talk in any length at a gathering or get into much detail about what you do and the needs of your client by emails and online postings, you should meet first and then try to set up a phone conversation. Here are a few tips.

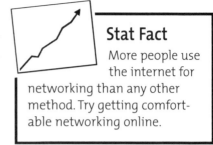

Stat Fact
More people use the internet for networking than any other method. Try getting comfortable networking online.

- listen more than you talk when you're on the phone with them
- listen for the first half of the conversation and try not to interrupt
- ask lots of open-ended questions that let the person speak their mind
- become so in demand that they all call you.

In the end, I know it's still scary to ask for the sale. But it's something you need to do.

These people are either going to say yes, or say no. I don't care if they say no! I would rather have a yes or no answer than to always wonder where they stand. More often than you may think, they will think the world of you, and will genuinely want to work with you. In the end, though, most customers will also want to hear you ask for the sale.

It's a strange phenomenon, but often someone who wants to buy something will not buy that something unless the salesman actually encourages them to buy it, and actively asks them to buy it. I guess it's a confidence thing—people want to buy from those who are confident about what they are selling.

Ask for the Sale

Therefore—and there's no way around this—you absolutely, positively need to ask for the sale. Fortunately, it is as simple and direct as, "Does this sound like something you would like to do?" They usually say yes. Then you simply say, "Okay, great! When do you want to get started?"

If you ask those two questions enough, you'll make sales. I promise.

Wrap Up

It's true, potential clients are all around you. BUT, you need to use some professionalism to attract them. Coaching takes a commitment on their part to not only

▲

work with you, but more significantly to open up and share details about themselves with a stranger. Therefore, you can't use cold calls or walk around wearing a sandwich board. You're not selling widgets or pretzels. You are selling a service that requires trust.

You need to carefully get the word out there via ads, flyers and brochures as well as on the Internet through your own website and writing for other people's websites. You also need to become proficient at networking, which means face to face or online. The goal is to talk to people, let them know what you do and listen to what they need. You then want to ask for the sale, or in this case, whether they would be interested in motivational of life coaching.

Deciding How Much to Charge

Deciding how much to charge is often one of the most difficult decisions you have to make as a new service provider. To be perfectly honest, your best bet may in fact be a form of trial and error.

On one hand you do not want to charge too little because you want to be in the professional range of coaching. Don't forget to check out the going rates in your area if you are mostly seeing people in person and in your niche if you have one. On the other side of the coin you don't want to charge too much and make it difficult for people who may want to see you on a frequent basis. Your goal is to find a comfortable price for your target market. This may vary depending on the types of people you attract. If, for example, you are coaching many young and/or struggling, artists, you may charge less than if you are coaching many top executives or attorneys. Know how much your target audience makes and can spend.

Trial and Error

I personally do not want an overload of clients, precisely because I need my free time to work on my own projects. At the same time, I need enough clients to keep the bills paid and to provide some rainy day money as well. For these reasons, I charge about $125 per hour. This keeps the number of clients low, but the bills paid at the same time.

Yes, for a lot of clients, this is too much. Yet for others, it is surprisingly reasonable. All in all, I get a response of about half and half; half would like it less expensive, and the other half would actually still pay if it were more expensive. And once I get my law degree and pass the bar exam, I might even consider going even a little higher. Time will tell, and that's exactly my point; things are going to change for you; things are going to change for your clients; and in the end, it is always going to be a matter of trial and error.

The key to remember is that if absolutely no one tells you that you're too expensive, then you are certainly not charging enough. On the other hand, if you find that lots of people seem interested, but never take the plunge, you may be charging way too much given where your reputation currently stands.

You see, I didn't start out charging $125 per hour. When I first started my company in 2000, I began by charging $50 per hour. And the hourly rate I would charge fluctuated between $50 and $150 for a long time until I finally discovered that $125 per hour is a happy and satisfying medium.

Smart Tip

Tip...

You've got to be really flexible with your prices in the beginning. It may take a while before you figure out what is best for your market.

Beware!
You cannot charge what you think you're worth; only what others think you are worth, and are willing to pay.

I was able to raise my rate to $125 because of my success as a coach. And your success in the field will provide you with the opportunity to raise your rates as well. The more credentials you amass as a coach will factor into your price, as does the institute in which you trained. If you studied with CTI or one of the other leaders in coaching, that too will factor into your rate.

While I was busy making movies, playing in a band and getting my Master's Degree, these were not reasons why someone should pay more for my coaching abilities. You don't pay your doctor a higher fee because he gets five strokes under par on the golf course do you? You pay more because of what he or she can do for you. Coaching is no different. As your education and experience in the coaching arena grows, you can continue to raise your rates . . . within reason of course.

Break-Even Analysis

Another tactic that will help you in determining how much to charge is to do a break-even analysis. I'll give you a quick schooling on the benefits of this tactic and you'll be able to use it not only for this current motivational coaching business of yours, but in every entrepreneurial venture you start for the rest of your life. Yeah, it's that useful!

How It Works

Break-even analysis is—in a nutshell—a simple way for entrepreneurs to determine how many sales they need to make to break even; i.e., to make a total net profit of $0. It also tells you at what price you should be selling your products or services to break even given a certain number of sales.

How does it work? Well, without getting overly complicated, here's the process.

1. Make a list of all the expenses your business is going to rack up during a typical month. This includes rent, payroll (i.e., to you!), cell phone, etc. Let's say $3,000 (and in reality, this should be a lot lower when starting out).

2. Take that number and divide it by the number of client sales you think you can make each month. Let's say you are feeling good about the future and decide 8.

3. Divide $3,000 by 8 to determine that each client is worth $375. Are you going to charge $375 per hour? Certainly not—at least at first.

4. Decide how many hours you think you can spend with each client each month or per coaching package. Let's say 5 hours over 5 meetings.

5. Divide $375 (from Step 3) by 5 hours to get an hourly rate of $75 per hour.

That's break-even analysis. Now you know that in order to break even each month (given $3,000 of expenses), you need to have eight clients, for five hours each, at a rate of $75 per hour, or sell eight five-week coaching programs for $375 each.

Putting It to Work

You can now do a number of different things with this information. You can actually offer an hourly rate of $75 per hour as a flat fee. Or, you can go ahead and offer a 5-hour package at $375. Or, you can offer a variation, such as 10 hours at $750, or 3 hours at $225.

Alternatively, you can raise the hourly rate above $75 and seek fewer clients, or you can reduce the hourly rate below $75 and seek more clients. As I said, it's all going to be a matter of trial and error to determine the best pricing and package strategy for your unique situation, and your break-even analysis is your starting point.

Personally, I don't like having single one-hour meetings because it's not a good use of my time. If I am going to run the credit card, set up a new client folder, take the time to get to know the client, etc., I want to be sure—up front—that this client is going to invest as much time into his own career as I am going to invest getting him into the system, so to speak. So I deal only in packages of five hours or more because then I only run the card once, and know that I have five hours now in the bank.

Your Bottom Line

What we just discussed here about break-even analysis is critically important because you just determined the *absolute minimum* you can charge (and how many clients you need) in order to break even. In other words, what we just calculated is how many clients you need, at what price, to ensure that your business stays afloat, that all the bills are paid each month, and that you go home each month with enough of a paycheck to survive.

How then do you make a profit and make lots of money? Simple: Sell more clients at the break-even rates you decided upon, and/or raise your break-even rates but keep the same number of clients.

The idea is that you never want to drop below your break-even numbers for the month. When you're just getting started, it may be a few months, or even a year or two (or longer) before you break even consistently each month and start to show a profit. That's OK, and it's normal if that happens. This is why it's so important that you have some cash reserves set aside, or a line of credit, to help you weather the non-profitable months. A key to remember is that there are many different variables involved in determining how long it's going to take to get past the break-even point—and to the determined and patient entrepreneur go the spoils.

Creating a Financial Cushion

As I mentioned above, it is precisely for these reasons that you should be sure to have enough cash or credit on hand when starting to keep the business running for the first year, or at least the first few months, assuming you make no sales whatsoever. As you may know, the number one reason businesses fail is lack of cash flow, which means they couldn't pay their bills. Their business may have been the greatest idea in the world, but often the greatest ideas take the longest to catch on. If you don't have the financial cushion to keep the business running while your marketing engine revs up, you may also be forced to close up shop before you get a chance to really show the world your stuff.

On that note, I will repeat: Keep your startup expenses low—super low! Don't buy the fancy swivel chairs; use a metal folding chair. Don't pay $1,500 for a flashy website; pay a few hundred for a very simple three-page site to begin with or go to one of the many sites that let you create your own website such as Hostgator.com or GoDaddy.com. Don't go out and get a new office line installed; use your cell phone. You may feel like you're running your business out of a bedroom, and well, that's the whole point—you are! That's how you *want* to be feeling! The more money you can save on the front end, the longer you are going to be able to persevere until suddenly—voila!—your business has taken off and you're making a living solely as a motivational coach. How nice!

But even then, be careful. The moment when success begins to take hold is often the danger zone for many entrepreneurs because as the income grows, they allow unnecessary expenses to grow as well. Be on guard, and don't let your success spoil you rotten.

What Are You Worth?
Perception Is Reality

This is perhaps one of the greatest financial lessons I've ever learned in my life: It doesn't matter *what I think I am worth*; it only matters *what other people think I am worth*.

In other words, perception is reality. Not *your* perception—oh no. The perception of your prospective *clients* is all that matters. If they think you are worth $500 per hour, but you are charging $100 per hour, you are going to be one successful motivational coach! On the other hand, if you are charging $100 per hour, but everyone thinks you are only worth $30 per hour, then you are going to go out of business very quickly.

The Solution?

As I mentioned, a lot of pricing for a service business is based on trial and error. But there are things you can do to improve your perception to potential clients. Gaining credibility is important, to do so you may:

- Continue to go for additional coaching credentials or other credits that might resonate in your niche market. Letters after your name can be helpful as long as they are bettering you as a coach.

- Discuss the success you have had with one of your clients and ask him or her if you can make it public—perhaps you will not be able to use their real name if they are uncomfortable disclosing such information.

- Get testimonials from people with whom you have worked

- Speak at seminars, conferences or do webinars.

- Write about your coaching experiences

Dollar Stretcher

If you want to really stretch your dollars, take the time to learn about break-even analysis and basic financial statements. It's amazing how many entrepreneurs start a business without knowing these basic skills.

A Balancing Act

Bottom line: Open your eyes and your ears; watch what people are doing, and listen to what they are saying. If you aren't securing a lot of clients, part of the reason (we'll cover other reasons later) is that you are probably charging too much—right now.

Just because no one will pay $500 per hour to meet with you now does not mean that in a few years, once your business is established and you are renowned the world over as the finest motivational coach in the world, people won't change their minds and decide that you *are* worth it.

Or, in a strange reversal, maybe you are not charging *enough*. It is possible that if your rates are too low, prospective clients will think you are not experienced enough to charge more.

On the other hand, maybe people are being scared off by your *low* price. Strange, but it just might be true. If you have really amazing credentials, but are charging below what others would expect to pay for that type of coach, they won't hire you because they'll think something must be wrong.

The pricing game thus is a true balancing act. On one hand you want to charge what you're worth. On the other hand, you're only worth what others say you are worth. We can boil the two sides of the pricing scale down very simply:

1. Raise and lower your prices until you find the one that works.
2. *Constantly* improve yourself, and your business, until it is undeniable that you are worth more than the rates you are charging.

In the end, the ideal situation is this: When you tell a prospective client your high-priced rates, she says, "Oh, wow, I thought you'd be a lot more expensive." That's a sweet feeling. Work towards it.

Creating Coaching Packages

As I mentioned before, my recommendation to you is to set up coaching packages and to not sell your time by the hour. I know you may think that it's easier to get someone to commit to paying for just one hour instead of three, or five, or ten, but you'd be surprised how much easier it is to sell a package. Why? Because clients want to feel that they are getting involved with someone who knows exactly the solution for their particular situation. Truly, how much help can you provide someone in just one hour? In my opinion, when I tell prospective clients that I insist on consistency and commitment in anyone who works with me, they all nod their heads in agreement. Of course they are consistent and committed, right?

By offering only packages, it implies that you already have a plan of action in mind for them that will unfold gloriously over the weeks you'll be working together. It also implies that your clients have big huge problems that only an extended package of meetings can come even close to solving.

Packaging Your Time

Of course, you want to make sure that when you offer a package, you actually do have a wonderful, magnificent, and inspiring course of study to draw on during all those meetings. You don't want it to be a haphazard collection of hourly meetings with no synergy between them. You need to be able to sell what you are going to deliver, but you also need to be able to deliver exactly what you just sold.

By offering packages, it makes your life easier too. Instead of running a credit card five times for five hourly meetings, you do it once, before the first meeting, and then you don't have to worry about chasing the client each week for payment.

Now you can breathe easy for five weeks, knowing that a full five hours worth of coaching fees are in your bank account for the month. It means that you are free to focus on the job of coaching that client, and not the sales process.

Making It Easy to Choose

Whether you decide to work on an hourly basis or through packages, you need to make it simple and easy for a prospective client to make the buying decision. If you offer four different packages and three different hourly rates, you are probably going to scare off potential clients with too many decisions. They are going to want to think about it.

Tip...

Smart Tip

It is usually easier to sell a customer a single package than five individual coaching sessions.

You don't want them to think about it. You want them to sign up now—today. And it's a heck of a lot easier for them to make a decision when they have an easy choice. Instead of having to answer two questions—Do I want to do this? If so, which package?—you make it easy for them by only requiring them ask one question: Do I want to do this?

You might think that by giving potential clients an a la carte choice of whatever they want would make it more likely that they'll find something that works for them. The opposite is true. They'll be confused, they'll begin to doubt themselves, and then—BOOM—you lost the sale.

Keeping It Simple

The reason most people are coming to you is precisely because they are having trouble making decisions. If you then give them a huge choice of options, you're just going to compound their confusion and fuel their doubt. Not a good move for a salesman.

Just imagine the difference in time it takes for you to pick out a cereal at a mini-mart at a gas station, as compared with how long it would take you at a supermarket. The selection at the mini-mart is so small that you make the decision in less than ten seconds. At the supermarket, you stroll up and down the aisle, comparing different flavors, colors, sizes, prices. Before you know it, the place is closing for the night and you still don't have tomorrow's breakfast.

Well, that's exactly what you do when you give your clients too much of a choice: They don't decide. They get scared, they feel nervous, and there is no way they will feel comfortable making a decision.

Beware!
Offering too many options is a mistake. Have you ever heard the expression, "Rejoice, Rejoice, You Have No Choice!"? That's exactly what I'm getting at. Customers will more likely buy if they don't have the complicated decision of choosing which package is best for them.

Down the line, once you're established, you can offer different options, but for now, one coaching package, or one hourly fee, is probably the saner, safer, and more profitable solution. The best part is that when the choices you give are so simple and clear, it makes your brochures, business cards, and website so much more powerful. You're in essence saying, "Hey, this is what I'm offering, take it or leave it." I know that seems counterintuitive, backwards, and not customer friendly, but I speak merely from experience. I have found that more people are willing to register for my coaching services when there is only one choice for them to make.

Wrap Up

In this section we looked at how much to charge. Most likely, just like myself, you will have to go through some trail and error to zero in on a rate that is neither too high or too low. Of course you will need to consider the going rate for coaching in your demographic market as well as for your target audience, especially if you are reaching out to a specific niche.

I then discussed the break even analysis which is how to determining the amount of money you need to earn to at least not lose money in your coaching practice. After a brief math lesson on how to put the break even analysis to work, I talked about the bottom line, which is the absolute minimum you could charge without losing money.

It's also very important to try to determine your perception of your own business and how it is perceived by others. Have you proven yourself a helpful coach to your clients? Can you get the word out about your successes in the coaching realm? It's important that you know your own value as a coach. There are also ways to increase your value, as discussed.

And finally we discussed packaging your time as a means of creating ongoing coaching sessions which benefits both yourself from a business perspective and your clients from the fact that they will have time to work on overcoming their obstacles and moving forward while trying to attain their own goals.

Profit
and Loss

Accounting is king! No joke. It amazes me how many books about how to start and run a business never talk about the absolute importance of understanding accounting. Frankly, it amazes me that I myself was able to keep my business afloat for over five years before learning about accounting. It's truly frightening, to tell you the truth.

Why is an understanding of accounting so important? The answer is clear: If you don't know where the money's coming from, where it's going, how much of it you have, and how much you owe—down to the last penny—then you really have no idea how your business is doing.

Some people call accounting the heart of a business; others refer to the financial statements as the report cards for a business; still others talk about accounting as a way to measure the health of a business. They are all right. And it behooves you to take whatever steps necessary to become a reasonable expert in accounting for the small business.

I'll get you off on the right foot with the following discussion of profit and loss statements, and balance sheets. In particular, I'll discuss how to use them when running your motivational coaching business. You'd be wise, however, to also pick up a few books on accounting and bookkeeping to continue your education. Your best bet, in fact, would be to enroll in an accounting course at your local university.

Income Statement

You probably already know what an income statement is, even if you don't realize it off the bat. In a nutshell, your monthly income statement is a measure of how much money is coming into the business each month, and how much is going out. It's a measure of income vs. expenses.

Now, you probably do some form of this already in your daily life. Perhaps you keep your receipts. Perhaps when a check comes in, you think how this new money is going to help you pay your bills, etc. Perhaps you keep track of expenses in a little notebook. (If you don't do any of these things, start! Please start!)

Well, an income statement is a formal way of consolidating all of these things, and it is crucial to prepare one each month in order for your business to operate at peak efficiency.

How to Prepare
an Income Statement

It's really simple to prepare an income statement each month. You need to keep track of every expense, no matter how little, each month.

1. At the end of each day, week, or month, tally up all the expenses, i.e., $200 for cell phone; $1000 for payroll to business owner (that's you!); $150 for advertising expense; etc.

2. At the end of the month, add up all of your business income for that month.

3. Subtract your total expenses for the month from your total (gross) income for the month.

4. The result is called the *net income*. If it's positive, you made a profit. If it's negative, you had a loss. If it's zero ($0), then you are breaking even.

Component Analysis

So, then, what do you do with this monthly income statement? It's time now to do something called *component analysis*, and yes, you are now getting a lesson on financial analysis.

Vertical Analysis

There are two types of component analysis: *vertical* and *horizontal*. Right now, with one month's income statement, you can only do vertical analysis, where you look at every expense as a percentage of gross sales for the month.

For example, if gross income was $3000, and office rent cost $1500, that means you spent 50 percent of gross income on rent expense—which is not good. It should generally be no more than 30 percent, and less if possible. With this information, you now know you need to do one of three things: increase gross sales next month, get rid of the office, or find a less expensive office space.

When you do this type of vertical analysis each month (with each expense broken down as a percentage of gross sales for the month), you'll start to realize which expenses are worth the expense and which are just sucking the profits right out of your business.

Horizontal Analysis

Next, once you get your second income statement completed (month two), you can then begin *horizontal* component analysis. This means that you now compare the same expenses as a percentage of gross sales over a period of time. For instance:

	Month 1	Month 2	Month 3
Gross Sales	$3000	$4000	$5000
Rent Expense	$1500	$1500	$1500
Rent Expense as a Percentage of Gross Sales	50%	37.5%	30%

In this example, once you can see the percentages, it is clear that the rent expense is becoming more manageable over time. On the other hand, if rent expenses were somehow going up each month while gross sales were also increasing, you might be surprised when you do the math:

	Month 1	Month 2	Month 3
Gross Sales	$3000	$4000	$5000
Rent Expense	$1500	$2000	$2500
Rent Expense as a Percentage of Gross Sales	50%	50%	50%

In this example, your gross sales are increasing, but so is your rent expense. Just by looking at the numbers, it's hard to tell exactly what's going on at a quick glance. But as soon as you do the horizontal component analysis, and then compare them across the various income statements, you can see that rent as a percentage of gross sales hasn't changed at all. You are still spending 50 percent of your gross sales on rent. Not cool.

Balance Sheet

The second financial statement you need to create each month is called the balance sheet. While the income statement is like a moving picture show of your business' health, the balance sheet is a photographic snapshot of how your business is doing at a certain point in time. Like the income statement, it is usually prepared once a month.

Like the income statement, the balance sheet also compares two variables, but instead of income and expenses for the month, the balance sheet compares the total assets of a company with the total liabilities of a company. In layman's terms, total assets is everything a company owns itself; total liabilities is everything a company owes to others.

The balance sheet, then, compares assets and liabilities. Specifically, it shows the difference between total assets and total liabilities, i.e., Total Assets minus Total Liabilities. The result is called your *equity*. Perhaps you are familiar with the universal accounting equation: Assets = Liabilities + Equity. It's just another way of explaining what the balance sheet is.

How to Prepare the Balance Sheet

Just like the income statement, the balance sheet is a simple thing to prepare each month. So how do you prepare it?

1. Add up the value of everything the company owns, i.e., cash in the bank, investments, inventory, real estate (even if you owe a mortgage), etc. These are your *assets*.

2. Add up the value of everything the company owes, i.e., credit card debt, bank loans, mortgage loans, etc. These are your *liabilities*.

3. Subtract your company liabilities from your assets, i.e., assets minus liabilities.

4. The result is your *net worth*. If it's positive, awesome! If it's negative, not as awesome. If it's $0, you're somewhere in between.

Vertical Analysis—Again

Now, what do you do with this balance sheet? Just like with the income statement, we can conduct both vertical and component analysis on it.

Vertically, we look at everything as a percentage of total assets. As an example, if total assets come to $7500, and total debt comes to $35,000, then your business debt is 466 percent of total assets. Expressed in another way, you have a total debt to total assets ratio of 4.6 to 1. This is definitely *not good*. Having some debt for the sake of leverage is sound business policy, but this is too much. 2:1, or even 3:1 would be more manageable.

Of course, you would have to look at your monthly income vs. monthly debt payments ratio to be sure if the total amount of debt is too much to handle. However, just by doing this simple ratio analysis, you have determined in just your first month that you have to increase your business assets and decrease your business debt by quite large amounts.

Horizontal Analysis—Again!

This leads perfectly into our horizontal component analysis of the balance sheet. Once you have a couple months' worth of balance sheets, you can begin horizontal analysis. Using the same example from above, let's take a look at three months' worth of balance sheets:

	Month 1	Month 2	Month 3
Total Assets	$7500	$5000	$1000
Business Debt	$35,000	$15,000	$1500
Business Debt as a Percentage of Total Assets	466% or 4.66 to 1	300% or 3 to 1	150% or 1.5 to 1

From this fanciful example, we see some very strange things going on. First, we notice that assets are dropping greatly every month. What does this mean? Part of that might be money being used to pay off the credit card debt. Or perhaps it is money being used to pay the ever increasing rent expenses when no income is coming into the business. We can't really answer that question fully without looking at the income statement for each of these months, and the rest of the balance sheet as well. That's fine, because the point of these analyses is to help ask the right questions and point towards potential problems.

Next, we notice that business debt has dropped to nearly zero by the end of month three. How did this happen? Again, there are many scenarios. Perhaps the business took out a bank loan at a lower interest rate to pay them off (in which case we should look at the rest of the balance sheet to see if that is indeed the case). Perhaps the company suddenly found a bunch of investors who wanted to help the business out of a huge mess. Who knows?

Questions, Not Answers

The key to remember with both income statements and balance sheets is that they do *not* provide answers; rather, as I mentioned above, they provide you with the right questions to ask yourself so that you can properly diagnose what is going on within your business.

> **Tip...**
>
> **Smart Tip**
> Buy a bunch of books on accounting, and enroll in a course at your local university. Seems like a big hassle right? I assure you that it's a much bigger hassle trying to run a company without understanding accounting.

Far too many entrepreneurs do not undertake this type of analysis, or they just let their accountant do it. Both scenarios are big mistakes. You are the CEO of your company, and it is your responsibility to figure out what is going on. They call it managerial accounting and financial analysis for a reason. As CEO, it is your responsibility to look at these financial statements and determine what you should be doing from a management standpoint to help the business reach and sustain profitability, and to eventually grow.

Tools for Preparing Financial Statements

Preparing your monthly financial statements is not something you can ignore. Did you read that last sentence? You absolutely must prepare your financial statements each month, and you absolutely must have a firm grasp of the basics of accounting and double-entry bookkeeping, otherwise you are flying your business on a wing and a prayer, and you're likely heading for a major crash.

Don't set yourself up for disaster! Set yourself up for success by learning the basics of accounting—read a few books on double entry accounting, and take a class at a local college.

 Beware!

Don't jump into Quickbooks without learning accounting and how to create financial statements. If you do that, you're just going to get lost and confused, and you're not going to understand what any of the statements mean. Trust me: Learning what Quickbooks is doing behind the scenes is important. If you don't know accounting, then you're not going to notice if something is askew with the statements.

Quickbooks

Once you *do* learn the basics of accounting and once you learn how to prepare your financial statements manually, the next step is to set up a computerized accounting system.

The one that I use is Quickbooks, and is probably the standard for small business owners who run their own businesses. The best part about using a computerized accounting system is that all you have to do each month is input your income and expenses from the last 30 days, and Quickbooks creates the financial statements for you. You just print them out, and analyze them! It's fantastic!

Quarterly Reports

After three months of inputting data into Quickbooks, you can use it to tally everything up to give you financial statements for the first quarter, like the big public companies do. Then, the financial statements for April, May, and June would be combined to provide second quarter statements, and so on, up until the fourth quarter.

Then begins Year 2. This is where things really start getting interesting. Now you can compare the financial statements from Month 1, Year 1 with those from Month 1, Year 2. You'll see some big lightbulbs go off when this happens. In other words, you'll be able to compare January of this year with January of last year, and see how things have changed, improved, or deteriorated. This is key information!

Eventually, you'll be able to compare First Quarter, Year 1 with First Quarter, Year 2. And the same with the Second, Third, and Fourth quarters.

Pretty soon, you'll be comparing financial statements from Year 1 with Year 2, and then Year 2 with Year 3. All along, you'd be looking for trends, unnecessary expenses, and anything else that might inspire you to improve the profitability and efficiency of your business.

Wrap Up

Absolutely none of this is possible if you don't learn about accounting and bookkeeping and introduce them into your business operations. Some say that they'll simply hire someone to do that for them. Big mistake. Have you ever heard stories of employees running off with all the money? It happens quite often in businesses where the head of the company doesn't understand accounting and bookkeeping. Please don't allow that to happen to you. Take the time to learn and understand accounting and bookkeeping now, before it's too late.

Running
Your Business

Believe it or not, starting the business is actually the easy part. The hard part is keeping it running. That is truly where the rubber meets the road. In many ways—and especially at the beginning—running your own business is just like having a regular job in that you have to do the same things every day if you want to succeed. For example, at a typical job, you have a routine that becomes a part of you, i.e., getting up at the same time, arriving at the same time, seeing the same people, etc.

Well, with your own upstart business—don't groan—you are going to have to do a lot of things in a very similar way in order to ensure that you *stay in business.*

Establishing Your Business Routine

Being self-employed, you will need to set up your own routine as a coach. There is no boss telling you what to do—so you're it.

Therefore, you need to set up a daily routine to make sure you accomplish the necessary tasks to keep your business running. Coaching, like all businesses, includes a number of business tasks. For starters you'll want to:

- Make sure to respond to e-mails and phone calls early on in the day, while you are fresh.
- You will want to do your online networking and look for places that you can go later in the day or in the week where you can network.
- You will want to make sure to handle all paperwork which ranges from bill paying to updating client files.
- You will also want to address any advertising or marketing plans you have started and follow-up on them. Make sure ads are placed appropriately and follow-up on responses from any advertising and/or networking.
- Finally, before seeing your clients for the day, you will want to double check your schedule and look over the files of any clients you will be working with in person or by phone.

Of course each person will adjust their routine to fit their own personal manner of getting things done. The key is to take care of the business end of your coaching business on a consistent daily basis.

Doing the Right Things at the Right Time

You see, one of the most often cited reasons for new venture failure is the inability to do the right things on a consistent basis—failure to do the things that need to be done according to a regular schedule.

On the flip side, if you make the effort to do the right things on a consistent basis, the success of your business is virtually assured. But here's the rub: What *are* those right things, and how consistent do you actually have to be?

Those are two very important questions, and the truth is—it depends. The right things for your business are going to be different perhaps from the right things for my business, and consistency for me may not end up being the same definition as consistency for you.

However—and this is a big however—that are certain rules that tend to be true for most businesses, and most certainly for a service business such as the one you are working on. Here are the top rules as I see them:

1. Network at meetings, gatherings, and over the internet. Meet people both on- and off-line.

2. Follow up with those who express interest. If it is huge interest, then follow up in a few days to a few weeks. If it is lukewarm interest, then follow up in a few months to a few years. If it is clear that they are not interested, put the name aside for now. People do change their minds so hold onto their information.

3. Follow up with past clients even more than potential clients. If they have come to you for coaching in the past, they are more likely to return.

4. Prepare your monthly financial statements religiously. Create them, print them, analyze them, and compare them. Do not forget them. They are critical.

5. Continually increase your expertise, and continually let everyone know about it.

6. Finally, every day, strive to learn something new about business, marketing, and finance—all disciplines that are going to help to keep your business competitive.

Finding Your Comfort Zone

You need to find your own comfort zone for your routine, or you're going to get burned out and quit following it. But you can't quit the routine! Just as Jay Levinson explains in *Guerrilla Marketing*, consistency is the key. If you want to run a successful business, then you absolutely positively need to be consistent in implementing your company's strategy. Until you have so much word-of-mouth referral business that you don't

Beware!
Don't create a routine that is so chock full of things to do that you end up not being able to follow it. Start with a manageable routine and add to it with time.

need to advertise anymore or network, you need to stick to the routine.

Often we hear of people quitting their jobs and starting a business because they didn't like being a slave to their boss, only to discover down the line that they are now slaves to their business. There's a yin and yang to that truth. First, in the long run, you certainly do not want to be a slave to your business—you don't want to just create another job for yourself. On the other hand, by becoming a slave in some respects to your business (i.e., by stubbornly sticking to your routine), you are setting the foundation for a successful business.

This latter point actually makes a lot of sense. Only by finding out what works, and then repeating those things ad nauseum are you ever going to be able to keep your business afloat. Don't get into this field thinking that this motivational coaching business of yours is just going to take off like a rocket. It probably isn't, and you're going to need to work your various systems day in and day out constantly in order to keep the money rolling in.

Prepare for Take Off!

If in the unlikely situation that your business does take off like a rocket, great! I hope in that case that you have a clear understanding of your various business, marketing, and financial systems that the sudden growth doesn't overwhelm you. In such a situation, the only way to avoid being overwhelmed is by first creating what I call your D.O.S., or demand overload strategy.

One of these days, whether on day one, or in year ten, if you are diligently implementing your routines on a daily basis, the hard work is going to pay off, and your expertise will be in sudden high demand. When this happens, you are either going to sink or swim. Those who sink do so because they weren't prepared. Those who swim to victory are those who already put into place the growth mechanisms (that D.O.S.) that they thought they'd never need; mechanisms such as hiring procedures for new staff, financial accounting systems that were ready for the growth, etc. If you're not prepared for huge growth, it could very well be your worst nightmare. If you're prepared, it'll be a walk in the park.

Therefore, in the short term, you need to work hard at creating duplicable systems and routines just to keep a steady stream of money coming into your business. In the long term, these very same systems and routines are what are going to make it easy for your business to expand and grow, and allow you to survive when you suddenly encounter a big increase in demand.

And truly, if you do manage to implement everything correctly, you are soon going to have such a huge demand for services that you are going to be in a position to hire additional help. At that point, if you hire the right people, and implement the right systems—then, and only then, will you be able to ensure that you don't end up a slave to your business. Instead, your business will end up a slave to you, kicking off income every week with a minimum of effort, allowing you to finally live the good life. Ahhh…

Maintain an Outside Income

If there is one thing I would have done differently when I started my business, I would have set up job security. In other words, I would have kept my day job as I worked and developed my new business. At the time, I was working as a temp at Morgan Stanley in New York City. I really didn't like the job at all. I was working the midnight to 8 A.M. shift three nights a week, and dealing with all of the silliness of corporate America. I was also making $20 an hour, which was nice, and a limousine took me home every night.

Unfortunately, when I decided I was going to start my new business, I figured it was going to be so easy to make the same, if not more, money—and by doing half the work—that I just quit my temp cold turkey after only the second week of being an entrepreneur. You see, I opened the doors of my new business, and during those first two weeks, I indeed patted myself on the back because I snagged two clients, paid up front, and woo hoo, I was going to be rich! So I quit my temp job, and put 110 percent of my time and effort into my new business.

That was my big mistake. After those first two clients, I realized getting new ones was a lot harder than it seemed at first. Now three weeks had gone by—and no new clients. What the heck! But I was so sure that more clients would be right around the corner, and I stubbornly stuck with it.

In the end, of course, it worked out, but those first three years were painful. And looking back, I realize that the smarter choice for me would have been to keep the temp job, but just cut back on the hours.

Beware!
Often would-be entrepreneurs are so excited to get started, and so optimistic about their future, that they foolishly quit their day job and devote all their time to their new business. Don't do that. You are going to need that steady source of income from the other job to help fuel your new business.

Move Fast, But Take Your Time

Despite your desire to start your own business and be free of "the man," don't rush into this. Take your time. Establish yourself first.

I guarantee you that you can run your new motivational coaching business part-time as you are getting started. Your website will be working for you 24/7. Worst case, at the end of each day, you can call any prospectives who contacted you from the website and set up a time to chat that's convenient for the both of you. You can set up your client meetings for after work on weekdays, during your lunch breaks, or anytime on weekends.

I assure you that you do not need to devote your every waking hour to this new business, and you shouldn't, because you want and *need* some sort of cash flow in the meantime. Truly, you are going to feel so relieved to see that paycheck from your day job during this first year getting your business off of the ground. If you follow this advice, I think you'll be glad you did.

One day, yes, you'll quit your regular job. I promise! And that will be a momentous day. But make that day a day when you really don't need that job anymore. Don't quit just because you *think* your business is going to take off—that's wishful thinking. Quit your job only when you *know*—by looking at your financial statements—that your business *has* taken off, and shows no signs of slowing down. Look at quitting your job as a reward—a reward for successfully creating a profitable entrepreneurial venture.

Wrap Up

Opening the business, while admirable, is not the end. It's in fact just the means. Once you are open for business, the hard part truly begins. Now it's time to start running your business. Just remember this truism: Starting a business is easy; keeping it running is another thing entirely.

Improving
Your Offerings

Once you've begun to establish yourself, you might then want to consider offering additional coaching packages to your clients. Once things get going, you might find that offering more options may make sense.

For instance, you might want to consider three-hour packages for those who are hesitant or short on cash, or instead, 12-hour packages for those who want to save additional money (i.e., give them a discount for buying in bulk.) You might also consider working on a per proj-

Smart Tip

Don't sell hourly meetings. Sell long-term packages!

Tip...

ect basis for a flat fee, or as you become more successful, perhaps via a flat monthly retainer that the client pays whether they use the time or not.

Option! Option!

You can see from these examples how things can expand and develop as time goes on. The more chances you take, and the longer you run your business, the more opportunities you will see and want to experiment with.

Of course opportunities to make money are always terrific, but you'll need to remember that your goal as a coach isn't simply about making money. There are certainly higher paying professions out there. As you think of ways to expand your business you need to do so with the mindset of helping people succeed and meet their goals. If you forget about the best interest of your clients you may be treading on "charlatan" territory.

That being said, you may also find instances in which you are coaching an individual on a specific project. In such instances you might work on a commission basis, putting yourself in there with your client. If for example, they win the grant or sell the screenplay, you get a percentage as a commission, if not, you, like your client, walk away empty handed. This can work to motivate people as they are in it for both of you.

However, this will only work in specific situations and with certain clients. If you decide to personally manage a client, keep in mind that you should be skilled in that area and not making it up as you go along. Be careful that if you take on other roles, make sure that you do not move into a conflict of interest.

Also, remember that you can do coaching by telephone. Believe it or not—it works. I have clients from sea to shining sea, and you can be sure I don't fly out to L.A. and Chicago each week to meet with them. I just do it by phone. It's the same price that everyone else pays, but more convenient for those who aren't in my particular metro area.

Back to Bill by the Hour?

As I mentioned earlier, I don't really think offering services by the hour is in your best interest. Building a successful coaching practice requires commitment on behalf of both the coach and the clients. If my clients are not willing to invest both their money and their time, I don't want to work with them. For these reasons, I do not recommend an hourly coaching rate.

Hourly fees work in many fields, most notably the legal field, where hourly fees, or "billable hours," are in many cases the norm. The difference, however, is that with legal fees, you don't often have a choice; you have to pay their fees, or their representation stops, and you are left to fend for yourself in whatever legal battle you may be enjoined. With motivational coaching, though, it's more of a privilege than a necessity.

Sure, you and I both know that the services we provide are actually a necessity (if the clients really are serious about becoming and staying successful), but when push comes to financial shove coaching falls to the bottom of most people's list. So if you charge by the hour, and your client's financial situation suddenly tanks, instead of paying you more money to help you fix the situation, they will usually drop you until their situation resolves.

This typically doesn't happen, however, when clients have already paid you for a certain number of hours. If you're doing your job correctly, over the course of their coaching package you should be able to keep tabs on their financial situation and help guide them towards improving that situation if it needs attention.

That all being said, if you want to try billing by the hour, why not? Maybe it will work for you. Just go into it knowing that it may make things more difficult, even though you may think it will help you get more clients in the short run.

In-Person Courses and Seminars

OK, so you've got your one-on-one coaching programs all set up. It's now time to consider in-person seminars. You'll want to consider them in two ways: first, as a stand-alone add-on to your coaching services, and second, as a lead generation tool as well.

Because of the dual purpose of your in-person seminars, you need to price your seminars and workshops very carefully. Charge too much and no one will show up. Charge too little, and you lose money on the seminar itself.

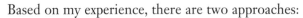
Based on my experience, there are two approaches:

First, plan some seminars that require attendees to pay. The idea is to charge something to help cover your expenses, but not so much that it scares people off. This way, you do make some money on the seminar even if no one ends up signing up to your coaching programs. However, if you play your cards right, you'll actually make a decent amount of money on your seminars, and then, make some real money by having people register for your coaching program as well.

Second, do not immediately turn down free opportunities to speak. While colleges pay me handsomely to speak at their schools, when AFTRA (the American Federation of Television and Radio Artists) asked me to speak to their membership with no fee, I eagerly said yes. The opportunity to speak to AFTRA members is too good to pass up, because many of them may indeed become my clients. Those who don't may at least spread some positive word of mouth. Finally, the credibility boost that I gain by speaking there can't be quantified.

Of course, on the flip side, you can charge an arm and a leg for your seminars if you want, but the seminars would not act so much as lead generation tools for your coaching services; they would be ends in and of themselves. In this case, your marketing will have to be even stronger, because the more you charge, the more work you have to do to justify the cost to your potential attendees. It's always amazing how a free seminar typically fills up to capacity, but a pay-for seminar always has empty seats. One is excellent as a lead generation device; the other is great as an income producer. But it's always easier to market the free seminars, for obvious reasons.

Hours and Groups

The length of each seminar will help you determine its goal. If it's a three-hour seminar, it is probably best used as a lead generation tool for your business. If it's a two-day weekend extravaganza, then it is probably leaning more towards a stand-alone money maker.

Something else you may want to consider is group coaching. In this case, it's a group setting, but instead of teaching, you are doing coaching with the group. In other words, you might have five or six people in the group, and you all meet perhaps once a month for three hours, and you go around and help facilitate their dreams and projects through questions, group interaction, and group projects.

This is a very interesting phenomenon because what it allows you to do is provide six to eight hours of coaching in only two or three hours a month. In other words, you're actually increasing your hourly rate, even if you end up charging less per person for the group coaching program. And that's a beautiful thing.

Wrap Up

A whole book can be written on this subject of seminars and group work, but here is what I want you to take away from this section:

- In-person seminars and workshops are immeasurably useful as both lead generation tools, and also as stand-alone money makers, depending on your goals.

- Your coaching practice as a whole will be more successful if you offer these group speaking engagements on a regular basis.

- Remember that you can do in-person seminars in places other than your home town. Thanks to your website, you will have fans in other cities. When you receive an email from a huge fan in another city, you might want to interview them on their interest in becoming your point person in that new city. Often the only way I am able to teach a seminar in a new city is by enlisting the help of someone who actually lives in that city—someone who helps me find the venue, promote the seminar, and assist in registering attendees.

Keeping Those
First Clients

Your clients are the most important thing in your business. Without them, you don't make any income. You not only need people to buy from you, you need them to buy repeatedly from you.

Stat Fact
It is easier and less expensive to keep a current client than to sell to a new client. Overall business statistics show that 80 percent of business comes from repeat customers.

Your client relationship, therefore, must be one of your highest priorities, because those first clients are not going to stick around if you give them reason to leave. You may be offering many reasons to stay, but if they perceive even one good reason to leave, they probably will.

And remember, a reason to leave may have nothing to do with you, per se. A reason to leave may end up being tickets to the ballet. Remember: You have more competition than just other coaching firms. You have to compete with every other business that might take that money away from your business. In other words, you have to make the client believe that their relationship with you is worth more to them than any of those other things. If you don't, your clients will leave.

Current Clients are Better Than New Clients

Beyond this, getting a client is a lot harder than keeping one. Strangely, people put lots of effort into getting clients, but then do so very little to keep them. And that's not such a smart move. Once you secure a client, treat them like princes and princesses.

If you have successfully enticed them through the door, your mission now is to keep them in that door. Not in a devious way of course but rather in a manner that is helpful to them. The more you help them reach their goals the more likely they will return. If you can provide first rate coaching services they will want to continue working with you. This means being attentive to their needs 24/7.

Of course, you're not expected to actually cater to your clients' every whim at every waking moment, but the more you let them know you care (and more than anyone else), the more likely they are going to stay by your side. It might be as simple as sending them a birthday card on that special day, or as complex as arranging a meeting for them with someone who they have been trying to connect with. Bottom line, you just want to do everything you can to keep your clients happy.

Customer Service

While we talk in more depth in a future chapter about the various systems you need to set up and employ to ensure that you keep those first clients, there are some generic customer service principles that we should focus on first.

Let's first be clear: You're going to be spending a lot of time up front trying attract those first clients. Most of your efforts are going to be spent on this. However, what happens when you finally get one? The first step: Celebrate! Congratulations! The second step: Stop celebrating right now and start holding on to them for dear life, because that first client is your food, your gas, your rent—your business. From that point on, you need to do everything you can to keep them.

For starters, you need to:

- Respond to their phone calls promptly.

- Respond to their emails promptly.

- Always ask if there is anything that they are unhappy with that you may be able to improve. Never ask, "Is everything going well?" Don't give them a leading question that forces them to say yes. Give them every opportunity to complain! The only way to save a sinking ship is if you first know that it is sinking!

- Establish an extended program of about five weeks for your client, as I recommended earlier. If you are able to do this, bravo, because now you have five chances to help them, instead of just one. Each of those five client meetings is an opportunity for you to set the stage for the next sale, and this is much better than selling individual coaching sessions by the hour.

- Document what you've helped them to accomplish, and show them. Better yet, have them make a similar list—a list of how they have changed, developed, and improved as a result of working with you. Often this exercise will help clients to realize for themselves that your services have been money well spent, because of their successes.

> **Tip...**
>
> **Smart Tip**
>
> Just because a client does not want to continue working with you now, does not mean they do not want to continue working with you later. Therefore, it is up to you to follow up with past clients. Selling them on a repeat package will be a lot easier than selling someone else on a new package, guaranteed.

- Consider offering a "returning client discount" if they continue, i.e., if you charge $750 for a five-week program, then reduce it to $650 for any returning clients.

- Truly help them! Make it your mission to do whatever it takes to go above and beyond what your clients ask of you.

- Finally, ask for the repeat sale. Don't meekly say, "Well, we're done. If you want to continue, you know where to find me." No, no, no! Ask for the repeat sale! "Well, we've made great progress together. What are your thoughts on continuing for another six meetings? Would you like to do that at a reduced rate of $650, instead of $750?" Confidence sells, ladies and gentlemen! The more confidently you ask for the sale, the more likely you are going to close on that sale.

Beware!
Some clients are really annoying, and unprofessional, and make you want to cringe. While they say that 'the customer is always right," in some cases, I feel that "the customer is always right for some other business." Don't be afraid to turn away a client if you do not want to work with that person.

60/40 Rule

This is certainly just a partial list, but the point is clear; when you get that first client, the percentages shift. Before, you were spending 100 percent of your time attracting clients. Now that you have that first client, you should now be spending 60 percent of your time servicing your current clients (even if it's just one), and only 40 percent of your time attracting new clients.

The whole idea is that if you do a good job with each client, the second sale to that same client will be easier, and the third even easier. As you get more and more clients, the percentages should shift even more: 80 percent of your time with current clients; 20 percent of your time attracting new customers.

You might be asking, "But what if they don't want to continue right then and there, but liked the services provided?" Good question. Same answer: 60/40. Smile, and then ask them when they think they'd be ready to start up again, and offer to call them to follow up around that time.

If they say, "Three months," then you mark down in your calendar to call them back in three months. I have clients that come back and forth over the years. On for five weeks, then off for a year, then back on for five weeks, off for a year—a type of annual kickstart to put together a revised business, marketing, and financial plan for the new year.

Wrap Up

By now, your company is already up and running. In fact, you're now a part of that group of entrepreneurs who finally realize that running a business is a lot of fun, but also a lot of hard work. And at many times, running a business is a big drag! Welcome to the world of the entrepreneur.

And now that you are open for business, you have probably realized that the development of that business is truly where the rubber meets the road. The thing that is going to set you apart from the competition is how well you are able to keep your current clients with you. If you can become a master at this, your business will probably always be in the black.

13

Sales and Marketing
Systems

One of the keys to the longevity of your business, and how much money you actually end up making, has to do with how effective your sales and marketing systems are. If everything you are doing is haphazard, constantly shifting, and never standardized, you're driving down the wrong street.

▲

To sustain a successful company, there are certain things you need to be doing, and constantly, to ensure your business always has a steady flow of income. The first is that you need a never-ending steady flow of prospective clients; the second is that you need a never-ending steady flow of converted/engaged clients; the third is that you need a never-ending steady flow of repeat clients.

All of these three issues are resolved and sustained in different ways. Prospective clients result from an effective *client attraction system*. Converted/ Engaged clients result from an effective *client engagement/conversion system*. Finally, repeat clients result from an effective *client retention system*.

Set up and implement each one properly on a consistent basis, and you'll be well on your way towards great success as an entrepreneur. Fail to do this, and you risk certain failure.

Your Client Attraction System

Before you even have to worry about how to handle clients, you need to learn how to attract them. For many, this is indeed the hardest part: Bringing your services to their attention, and enticing them to make the effort to actually contact you. Phew! That's a tall order. And that's precisely why you need to have a proven, effective, and manageable client attraction system in place, and in operation.

To be sure, there are only two ways that you are going to attract anyone; either through advertising, or through publicity. That's encouraging, isn't it? Just two things you need to master.

Well, the bad news is that to master these two disciplines, it is going to take a lot of blood, sweat, and tears. Fortunately, since you don't have many clients when you're just starting out, you'll also probably have a lot of time on your hands to work on developing this crucial system for your business! Nice way of looking at it, right?

Stat Fact
The most successful businesses in the world are those that took the time to establish a set of systems that work.

Advertising and Publicity

So, what do you need to do? First, you need to learn the differences between advertising and publicity. I came up with a nice handy way to remember the differences a few years back called CCC, which stands for cost, credibility, and control. You see, advertising is high cost, low credibility, but high control, whereas publicity is low cost, high credibility, and low control. If you remember CCC, you'll always remember the differences between the two. Most importantly, you need to understand that the only way you are going to get low cost, high credibility, and high control is by using both advertising and publicity, simultaneously.

Second, you need to take some time and actually sit down with a pad and paper and *think*. Think about how you are going to attract your target market. Who *is* your target market? What magazines do they read? What newspapers? Who are the influential people in their field? Who do *you* know who knows people in your target market?

Don't think in terms of advertising and publicity. Say to yourself "What can I do to attract potential clients?" That's it. That's the only question you really have to worry about. If it were me, and I were just starting out, the answers would be:

- Give as many free lectures/seminars as I can.
- Talk to *everyone* about what I do.
- Pass out business cards everywhere, even to strangers.
- Wear a T-shirt that says, "Ask me what I do for a living."
- Call all of your friends and ask them for referrals.
- Consider taking out a small series of ads in the trade papers appropriate to your target market (doing your break-even analysis first, before making any rash decisions).
- Send press releases to the local press, and then call them.
- Check out Google AdWords and other pay-per-click advertising.
- Read *Guerrilla Marketing* by Jay Conrad Levinson.
- Read *Guerrilla Networking* by Jay Conrad Levinson and Monroe Mann.

Constant Implementation, Improvement, and Synergy

Once you have this list in front of you (and your list should be much longer than my list above), you're only halfway done. You see, creating the list was the easy part. The hard part is actually implementing these things, and then tracking the effectiveness of each one. After a while, you'll get a feel for what is working, and what isn't working. What works immediately is added to your system. What doesn't work is re-evaluated, and potentially retried again, but does not become a part of your regular system.

For example, for some entrepreneurs, Google AdWords is the answer to their prayers. With AdWords, you only pay when someone clicks on your ad and visits your website. This works very well for those who take the time to make sure their keywords and ads are directly related to the landing page on their website, and that there is a clear call to action on the website for a service that the people visiting actually need. If so, then your pay-per-click expenses will more than pay for themselves. The problems arise when the keywords do not properly correlate to the ads, and when the ads do not correlate to the website, and when the website does not have a clear call to action.

Do you see how important it is that everything in your publicity, marketing, and advertising (PMA) system is synergized? If one part of your PMA system is incongruous, the whole system won't work. AdWords is a perfect example of this, but it applies to every facet of your PMA system. The same applies to your brochures, to your business cards, to your print ads, and anything else you are doing from a publicity, marketing, or advertising standpoint: Some things will work; other things will not work.

This is why it is so important to continually improve upon your system by constantly experimenting with new forms of attraction to see which ones pull the most, in an effort to determine which tactics deserve to be a regular part of your consistently implemented system. It is sad that so many companies go out of business because they foolishly waste their money on advertising that doesn't pay.

Inexpensive Advertising

In both *Guerrilla Marketing* and *Your Marketing Sucks*, the authors explain the importance of only investing in publicity, marketing, and advertising that is inexpensive. For example, if you spend $10,000 on an ad campaign that brings in $50,000, clearly, that was inexpensive. On the other hand, if you spend $10, but only bring in $5, then that cost, even though a mere fraction of $10,000, is actually *more expensive*. Make sense?

If you make enough of these expensive mistakes, you're going to end up losing all your money and going out of business. While making mistakes and learning how to best make use of resources is all a part of being an entrepreneur, you just simply can't afford to continually make the same mistakes over and over again. Keep in mind:

- You have to experiment with low amounts of money and low investments.
- You can't blow your entire budget on an unproven marketing strategy.
- Whenever you can, you should be using low- or no-cost marketing strategies to lower your break-even point.

Finding the Right Marketing Mix

Of course, it may take time to find the best marketing mix for your business, but that's all part of the game. The bottom line is that you have to be willing to go to great efforts to find that perfect marketing mix, no matter how long it takes.

For instance, I didn't realize it until five years into my business that just by offering a free 20-minute career consultation, I would attract many more client prospects. And it wasn't until five years into my business that I realized that spending money on print advertising in newspapers was high cost with low attraction. Today I work primarily off of referrals; however, I can't deny that the reason I have a lot of clients taking me up on a free career consultation is because they knew about me initially from ads I once took out in newspapers. So it really is a matter of trial and error, and constant readjustment.

Don't go overboard with spending when you're just starting out. Start out slowly, keep your day job, and don't spend your life savings or max out your credit on full-page ads, expensive glossy brochures, or $3,000 websites. That—to be frank—is simply a huge waste of money. Remember: The profit is in the expenses! Or to be more precise—in the lack thereof.

Oh, and don't assume that just because a certain advertising or publicity strategy is not working for you that it will never work. It is quite possible that you are just not implementing the strategy correctly. This is a big problem with a lot of entrepreneurs; they try something on a lark, decide it doesn't work, and then disregard it as an option for all eternity. That's a big mistake. Don't let your ego get in the way; admit that it's possible that if you tried again, after learning more about the strategy, you might very well succeed.

Beware!
Do not focus solely on attracting clients. Often, the breakdown occurs after the attraction, during the sales process. Take the time to learn how to sell.

▲

Your Client Engagement/ Conversion System

Your next sales system—your client engagement and conversion system—kicks in once you've successfully attracted someone into your sales funnel. How did this happen? How did you attract someone into your sales funnel? This happened because your client attraction system is obviously working—perhaps not yet perfectly, but good enough to have drawn someone in. Good job!

Now that your client attraction system brought them in, your next step is to engage them one-on-one, and convert them into a paying client. It's time to put that salesman cap on and dive right in!

Unfortunately, in many cases, this is where things fall apart for a lot of entrepreneurs. They were able to attract someone through solid marketing, but then lost the sale because of poor salesmanship—because of something they said or didn't say, or something they did or didn't do. It's time to engage that person and convert them into a client.

It's going to take a lot of trial and error before you figure out what works and what doesn't work for you. Throughout this whole entrepreneurial process, there are times when you are going to feel very disappointed, and probably want to throw in the towel. There's often nothing more frustrating and depressing than to attract someone and then not have them buy.

Here's some advice: Roll with the punches, and drive on. This is sales. It typically takes a heck of a lot of nos just to get to one yes. And that is what separates the winners from the losers. As long as you've got the backbone to handle some rejection, you're gonna do just fine.

Do's and Don'ts

To begin with, you want to make a list of all of the things you are going to do to potentially engage and convert prospects into clients. Your list might include:

- Display confidence when speaking with them.
- Don't say "um," "like," or "you know"—it makes you sound unprepared.
- Smile when speaking to them.

- Do more listening than speaking. Remember, coaching is about their needs, not simply about you making a sale.

- Make the other person feel at ease.

- Don't be a sleazy, pushy salesman.

- Explain to them why what you offer is exactly what they are looking for (but only after hearing exactly what it is they are looking for).

- Actually ask for the sale!

Beware!
You have to ask for the sale. Directly. looking in their eyes. With confidence. If you don't, you're leaving the success of your business to mere chance and that's pretty lame.

Once again, this list is only half the battle. The true test is after you put each bullet into action. Some of the strategies on your list you may find work great; others not at all. The only way to find out is by testing each one, and analyzing the results. Things that work are added to your system; things that don't work are re-evaluated and added later, or discarded. And then, try again with something new.

A good rule of thumb is that once you have a basic system in place, you should be spending 80 percent of your time implementing and working it consistently, and the remaining 20 percent of your time investing in new tactics and experiments. The whole idea is to create a business that runs completely on systems, so that eventually it can run on autopilot and you don't have to think too much—just execute. And that efficiency ultimately frees you up to do better things with your time—perhaps spending the money you are making while relaxing on a beach in Key Largo!

Your Client Retention System

Finally, the last part of your sales system is designed to ensure that once you attract and convert prospects *into* clients... that they *remain* clients. Thus the name: your client *retention* system.

It has been proven time and time again that it is easier to keep clients than it is to secure new ones. The reason is quite straightforward. Current clients have already been sold once; they already know and trust you; you are familiar. In other words, as long as you did a great job servicing them, you won't have to do as much work to convince them to buy again.

Now, your client retention system actually consists of two parts. Part one is how you interact and treat your clients *while* they are with you, and part two is how you interact and treat your clients *in between* servicing them. In other words, you want to do everything possible (as discussed above) to provide top quality service while you have your clients in your grasp. However, in the quite likely scenario where someone works with you briefly and then decides to take a break, you have to know how to handle that situation so that these clients come *back* to you.

Beware!
Do not become an annoying caller. You do not want to ever be called a telemarketer—you want to be a friend who is calling with the best interest of the other person in mind. It's not about you and making a sale; it's about your clients, and helping them to live better and more satisfying lives.

The key tactic for this situation: Follow up. And this technique is something that you will find equally as helpful in gaining new clients as in retaining them. All too often—and in most cases in fact—no does not mean no; it just means not right now.

In fact, according to life insurance sales statistics, it sometimes takes up to three entire years before someone becomes a client—assuming proper follow-up. Frankly, if life insurance can be successfully sold within three years, then you can certainly sell your coaching services in that amount of time as well.

No Only Means Not Now

Therefore, you might be wise to use a similar strategy with your sales system. Assume that even if people initially say no, it may take up to three years to prove to them that your coaching methodology really works. However—and this is a big however—none of this will matter if you do not have a way of tracking every single prospect, and every single client, that walks through your doors, sends you an email, or calls you on the phone.

The system that I use is called the *one card system* [OneCardSystem.com], and was designed for financial planners and insurance sales reps. Fortunately, with slight modifications, it works for any service business, and I enthusiastically recommend it for whatever coaching field in which you find yourself.

It's actually quite simple. Whenever a potential prospect contacts you, you create a yellow card for them in your card box, and gather pertinent info about them. Ideally, they become a client immediately, in which case you staple the yellow card to a new client folder that you just created for them, and then you make a white card and put it in the card box instead of the yellow. In other words, yellow cards are for potential clients, and white cards are for those who have actually purchased from you.

If however the potential prospect does not sign up immediately, no problem! You add the yellow card to the card box, and you follow up regularly using that yellow card. And when that yellow card prospect finally decides to become a client, you again staple that yellow card to a new client folder, create a new white card for this new client, and add it back to your card file. Quite simple; quite effective.

Follow Up!

So how often do you follow up? It depends. At minimum at least once a year, but depending on how eager the prospects are, and their particular situation, it might be wise to follow up every month, or perhaps even the following week. It doesn't matter. The point is that if someone has shown interest—that is solid gold. They may not buy from you today, and that's fine, as long as you remember to follow up.

You see, the key for you to remember is that they probably will buy from you if you follow up with them regularly with courteous, non-pushy, non-sleazy, and non-threatening phone calls. Yes, you have to pick up that phone. Emails are good and so are newsletters, but the rubber meets the road with the phone calls. It's scary, but when you have a good system in place, you realize that every phone call is money in the bank—even if someone says no.

Think Long Term

Too many entrepreneurs in service businesses take a short-term approach to client development. They assume that if the prospective client does not buy today, they will never buy. That's a big misunderstanding. The truth is that the majority of people who end up becoming clients probably will not trust you enough the first time you speak with them.

Therefore, to discard them because they didn't buy from you the first time is short-sighted and poor business. This is why you need such a clear and organized contact management system set up and in place. The majority of your clients are probably going to buy months or years later, and you will only see their business if you have the smarts to keep in touch with them regularly.

Of course, there will be cases where it doesn't even make sense to create a yellow card for someone, i.e. when it is clear that this person will *never* buy from you—and you'll know this person when you speak with him. For me, it's the people who I can tell are just looking for a quick fix; those who are obviously never going to see the value in what I

offer, or who make me feel unmotivated just speaking with them. Truly, just being on the phone with some people takes away all my enthusiasm and joy. That person doesn't stay in my card box.

Cut Your Losses

Similarly, after a period of three years, if someone hasn't returned any of your phone calls or showed any interest, you should probably discard that yellow card to ensure the leads in your card box are fresh and live. Having a box full of lukewarm prospects is a waste of time and efficiency. Give everyone a fair chance to realize how wonderful your services are, and then don't bother with them.

In other words, don't let bad leads slow you down. Tear up those sour yellow cards with full confidence, knowing that if those individuals ever change their minds, they can contact you again and you can create a new yellow card for them.

What about Your Current Clients?

Finally, this same procedure applies to your white cards, i.e., those who have actually become clients. If they work with you for a while, and then stop—that is not an excuse for you to stop keeping in touch too! You need to follow up with them just as you would your prospective clients; usually once every six months, to see where they are and if they need any help. Even if you don't hear back from them, continue to let them know that you care through your regular phone calls, newsletters, and emails.

The National Underwriter Company (who sells the One Card System) includes a wonderful (and huge) book with the full system that actually teaches you how it all works, why it all works, and how to make it all work for you. Of course, they are assuming that you are a life insurance sales rep/financial planner, but that is irrelevant.

In most cases, just put your own business in place of the one they discuss. Most of what they talk about is valid for any sales business, and frankly, as I said before, if it works when selling life insurance—which is really hard to sell—then it will certainly work for whatever you are selling as well!

Wrap Up

Have you set up your systems yet? Is everything organized? Are you on top of things? Have you been doing your accounting every month, and analyzing your financial statements? Have your first clients returned for more business? Are people referring you to their friends? Are the coaching services you are offering helping people? Are you asking for and receiving feedback? Are you acting on that feedback? These questions are endless.

The point is that starting a business is not the hard part; running the business successfully is the hard part. That is why I encouraged you earlier in the book to start your new business sooner rather than later—you don't need as much practice starting a business as you do running a business. So if you haven't yet started your business, now would be a good time!

14

Making
a Profit

Certainly, the whole point of going into business goes beyond just not losing money, but eventually into making money. Many new entrepreneurs (and even some who have already been in business for a while) incorrectly think that just because they are making sales and that cash is flowing into the business, that they are making money.

While it may be true that there is money changing hands, it is quite possible that you are actually losing money at the end of each month.

You really don't know if you are actually making money—a phrase that is often synonymous with making a profit—until you first establish your break-even amount. After that, it's a simple matter to determine if you are making a profit. Did you bring in gross sales greater than your break-even amount? If so, you just made a profit.

Breaking Even Is Only the Beginning

This may seem like a simplistic point I am making, but actually, it's of significant importance. If you just break even every month, it means you are not expanding. It means you are not growing. In fact, if you did not include your own paycheck in the upfront expenses, and you just break even, it means you yourself do not even make any money. And that's not a good thing. You simply must move beyond the break-even point.

And here's the rub: First, it is really *really* hard just to break even each and every month. Hitting the break-even point itself is a major challenge (and accomplishment). But unfortunately, that's just half the battle.

Once you hit the break-even point, that's when you really have to kick your afterburners on in order to push beyond—to the point of growing, and sustainable, profitability.

Getting to Profitability

How do you get to a point of growing and sustainable profitability? How do you get to the fantastic point of moving beyond breaking even?

It's a combination of things. First, you need to understand accounting and bookkeeping, as we discussed previously. Second, you need to be working to reduce your expenses at every juncture. Think about it: The lower your expenses each month, the easier it becomes to hit the break-even point, and the easier it will be to become profitable. Third, you need to consistently be improving the quality of your products and services. You need to be consistently tweaking (and implementing) your PMA strategies. You need to be consistently picking yourself up each time you get slapped around and slammed to the ground—and yes, that is *going* to happen.

The Three Bells

Remember: On average, a typical entrepreneurial enterprise takes from two to five years to become profitable. This statement should ring three bells in your head.

First, it should be encouraging! Yes, it takes time for a business to take off! That's OK—it's normal.

Second, it should make it clear to you that you unequivocally need another source of income during those first two to five years to cover your personal and business expenses until that profitability kicks in. This may be money you've saved up over the years, a business loan or line of credit, or most likely (and my personal recommendation), a part-time job that pays the bills.

Third, it should act as a constant reminder that it takes work to become a profitable business. Lots of blood, sweat, and tears; lots of sacrifice and lots of determination and discipline. Never start a business with the misconception that it's going to start earning a profit from day one. While that may happen, of course, it is certainly not the norm for that to happen. Which segues nicely into our next topic: Business savings accounts.

Business Savings Accounts

While it is every entrepreneur's dream to never have to struggle or lose business, economic history has proven that downturns happen to the best of us. To that end, the best entrepreneurs are those who have money saved in a business savings account for just those rainy days.

As an entrepreneur, you are not on salary. You cannot expect the same paycheck every two weeks as you would from a regular job. Perhaps once you are fully established, you can put yourself on a regular paycheck, but when bootstrapping a business together from the ground up, some months you may make $5,000, and others you may make absolutely nothing. It is good to have money in the bank during these periods.

Moreover, since you can't plan for every single emergency (or investment opportunity), it is not only smart, but downright essential, that every entrepreneur keep at least three months of expenses in a savings account at all times. That money is there for two reasons: First, to act as an emergency buffer for unexpected expenses, such as if suddenly rent jumps up, or taxes are more than you expect, etc.; and second, to act as an emergency investment fund, for when some great investment opportunity comes along.

Funding Your Business Savings

First, you can transfer the money from your personal savings account into your new business account. Or, if you don't have enough personal savings, you can do it the old fashioned way by paying yourself first, or in this case, by paying the business first. In other words, when you get your first paying client—let's say at $500 for a 5-week program—you would take the first 10 percent out immediately and put it into your business savings account. In this case, you would take $50 off the top and deposit it into your business savings account.

Ideally, this business savings account would be the one affiliated with your business checking account. While the interest rate is very low, the really nice thing about linking the two is that typically the savings account then can become a non-credit based overdraft protection. This is what I do, and it's great; it encourages me to continually add money to my business savings account, and it also acts as a safety net.

Raising Additional Capital

At some point, you are going to need money to expand. It may be a lot, or it may be a little, but in order to expand, you are going to need money. And you probably aren't going to have it. It is called mezzanine funding—basically it means your company is doing really well, but in order to expand, it needs an infusion of cash that you currently don't have.

Fortunately, mezzanine funding is easier to raise than startup capital. In this situation, you've already proven the business model to be successful, and you've proven yourself to be a competent CEO. In this scenario it is clear why s would be more likely to provide you with money.

In fact, at this point, if the business has been in operation for at least three years—and assuming you've been diligent with your accounting (and assuming you are now making a profit)—you'll have three solid yearly profit and loss statements, and one solid balance sheet. You can take those P&Ls and balance sheet to any bank, along with a business plan outlining your plans for expansion, and you very well may be offered that loan you were trying to secure when starting out.

Of course, if your business is extremely profitable, there is a possibility that you won't have to get a loan, or even find investors; you can re-invest the profits from the business into the expansion. The beauty of this is that you won't have to owe anything to any bank or investor.

Trust

When trying to convince others to invest in your company, there is only one thing that will entice them to do it: Trust. If they believe that they will—at the very least—see their money again, they will invest. The only way anyone will believe that they will see their money again, though, is if they trust the management team. That trust comes from a combination of experience, past success, honesty, full disclosure, your partners, your confidence… and the list goes on.

The point: If you want to expand, you need to do whatever it takes to get your potential investors to trust you. If they do, they will—quite simply—give you their money.

If you can convince investors that they are at the very least going to see their money again, you shouldn't have any difficulty at all convincing them to help you out. Further, if you can then convince these same investors that they are going to end up with lots of additional money beyond just getting their original investment back, then you just might have to turn investors *away*. I truly hope that is the situation you have to face.

Wrap Up

Every startup entrepreneur's mission should be to reach stabilization as soon as possible.

Making a profit is the first part of stabilization, and making a profit consistently is the true measure of stability.

Stabilization is not something that you should start thinking about many years into the success of your business. No, stabilization is something that you should start thinking about on the day you *open* your business—because the sooner you can stabilize everything, the sooner your stress levels are going to go down, and the more in control you are going to be.

Company Operations Handbook

A company operations handbook? Why would a one-person firm need that? Well, first, I certainly hope that your company is not going to remain a one-person firm for long. More importantly, you need a company operations handbook because the more you can streamline the things you do into routine tasks that you can write down, the easier it is going to be for you to run your business in a standardized manner. And the sooner your day-to-day and month-to-month tasks are standardized and uniform, the sooner you can start to put your business on auto-pilot—which means you will start to have more free time to spend elsewhere, and you'll have more time to work on expanding the business.

Perhaps even *more* important, having a company operations handbook will help reduce your stress by giving you a plan for you to use each day. Instead of you working the plan, the idea is that the plan will start to work *you*. You won't have to think as much anymore; once you have an effective operations handbook in play, the only thing you'll have to remember to do each day is open up the handbook and do what it says!

Assembling Your Magic Handbook

As you can imagine, coming up with this magic handbook is not an easy task. It is going to take you a long time to fully determine what works, and what doesn't. The only tasks and duties that should ever end up in your company handbook are those that you know to be effective.

In other words, experimental advertising initiatives should not be included. However, if you know that spending $50 on a small ad in a trade journal each month brings in hundreds of prospective clients, then certainly that should become part of the standardization of your company. Yes, it's all trial and error, but *well-researched* trial and error.

Therefore, assembly of your operations manual should be something you begin doing from day one. It is certainly not going to be completed on day one, but this operations manual is not going to be complete on day 10, or day 100, or day 5000 either. You see, it is and should always be a work in progress. While the tasks and duties in the most current handbook will always be the current standard, the idea is to always be experimenting with other possibilities in an effort to continually improve.

Smart Tip

Tip...

With a good operations manual and a trustworthy staff, you can become one of those owners who just receives the checks, but doesn't actually run the business. Something to consider unless of course you are a coach who really wants to help people.

Remember, you always want to spend the majority of your PMA budget on things that work; i.e., put the majority of your budget into the current standardized plan. The remaining cash should then be put into experimental initiatives.

When you first start your business, you're going to be running around like a chicken with its head cut off—crazy, hectic, scared, and confused. Your mission from day one should be to re-attach your head as soon as possible and to regain a measure of control and formality. This is where the handbook comes in.

In Case of
an Emergency . . .

Of course, another key reason to begin establishing your operations manual from day one is to act as a security blanket for when that big freeze comes in. Inevitably, there will come a time when you have no idea what to do, or when you didn't expect something to happen.

Well, the whole idea of this operations manual is to help plan for exactly these types of problems. Since you are putting the manual together while you are feeling confident and in control, the idea is that if suddenly you become scared, freaked out, or confused, you can turn to the operations manual—which should be chock-full of proven tasks that will keep you moving forward, despite your stress, confusion, or depression.

Create a
Problem-Solver List

In addition, part of the manual should include an emergencies section that includes potential problems, and what you are going to do when they occur. For example, some possibilities include:

Problem: Ran out of operating cash and bills are due.
Solutions: Use a credit card, negotiate with creditors, use emergency savings.

Problem: Overload of client demand.
Solutions: Schedule overload into following month, hire additional coaches, turn down some business.

Problem: Lack of client demand.

Solutions: Do more marketing and promotion, call all current clients and ask for referrals, take out an ad in the trade papers.

Problem: Bad publicity.

Solutions: Hire a good publicist who is good at spin control, send a press release, and make a public statement.

Of course, this is just a small number of the potential contingency plans you can have at your disposal, but the key is that you need to have this list of problems and solutions thought out *before* any of them come to pass. Many people fail in business because they think too short-term—they fail to plan what might go wrong, and they fail to plan what might go right. As a result, they are taken by surprise when those things do happen, and are thus not prepared to take immediate action to fix the problem or take advantage of the opportunity.

Your well-prepared operations manual will help ensure that you are never taken by surprise when something crazy happens in your entrepreneurial world.

Preparing for Change

Finally, your operations manual is the *key* to expanding your business. By expansion, I mean two possible things: Either expanding the company in its current location by hiring additional employees, or expanding the company in new locations entirely. Both situations require an up-to-date and standardized way of doing things, i.e., a current operations manual.

The reason you need an operations manual to hire employees is because it becomes the basis for your employee manual. Inside your operations manual, you are going to break down each "job" that you do into component parts. For instance, while you may do everything yourself when getting started, you have to realize that you are actually doing the jobs of about 20 people. You're the accountant, the publicist, the bookkeeper, the salesman, the CEO, the President, the Vice President, etc. Hiring just becomes a heck of a lot easier when you have job descriptions already written out and prepared.

Compartmentalize

The sooner you start to compartmentalize what individual roles you are actually playing, the sooner you will be able to troubleshoot and diagnose problems in your business by department. Rather than merely saying, "Something's wrong," you'll be able to specifically pinpoint that the issue is in your sales department, your accounting department, or your advertising department.

Smart Tip

Tip...

Running your business without an operations manual is like going on an arctic expedition without a map and without a jacket. Don't do it.

In addition, by compartmentalizing the jobs that you yourself are currently doing, you will then be able to siphon off the various jobs to other team members as the need arises, and as the business becomes more profitable.

Current Operations

This operations manual is useful even after employees come on board. First, it gives them a complete overview of how the company works from beginning to end. Second, it gives them a clear outline of what is expected of them as an employee. Third, it helps show them how their job relates and interacts with the other team members. This is truly invaluable to any employee.

Expansion

Finally, a standardized operations manual will allow you to easily open up additional locations in different cities. Hiring the right office manager for the new location is only half the battle; the other half is making it easy and efficient for this person to run the new location with minimum assistance from you in the home office. The more clear and standardized the manual, the more likely the branch offices are going to succeed. While each location may require unique adjustments, the success of McDonald's and other fast food restaurants proves that running each branch in virtually the same manner is a recipe for success across the board.

▲

Wrap Up

Without stabilization and standardization, you may very well find that instead of you running the business, the business is running you, and running you into the ground! This is why a company operations handbook is a big key to your success.

Of course, finding stabilization may take time. You are going to have to experiment with a lot of different things, and certainly make a lot of mistakes before you finally realize what works best. Perhaps most importantly, stabilization is the key to hiring others, expanding the firm, or selling it, all topics we'll discuss shortly. Without standardization that comes from stabilization, you're not running a company; you're flapping around with a company, just hoping to hit the right sales targets, and just hoping to flap into the right opportunities. That's not running a business; that's just wishful thinking and that's precisely just what you don't want to do.

Publicizing
Your Business

Unfortunately, just because you have accounting down pat, have the greatest customer service in the world, and are the best coach this side of Texas, if no one knows it then none of that really matters, does it?

As I repeatedly remind my clients, it is not your talent that makes you a star, but rather, the publicity of that talent that makes you a star, and keeps you a star. And if you want to expand, becoming a master of publicity is just the beginning.

In fact, this is precisely why there are so many movie stars who are bad actors; rock stars who can't sing; and best-selling authors who can't write. Why? Because it's not so much their talent that is keeping them at the top; it's their box-office draw, their ticket sales, and their book sales. People know who they are; they are famous and bigger than life, so people just buy their products and services in droves.

As hard as it is to believe, the reason these people are so successful is not because they are the best. They may be, but they probably are not. There are certainly better actors, singers, and writers out there. Unfortunately, though, all of those better actors, singers, and writers just don't know how to let other people know that! If they did, they would be the ones on the cover of *People* magazine.

Publicity, Marketing, and Advertising

The number one key to moving towards break-even status, then profitability, and finally expansion, is going to be your PMA (publicity, marketing, and advertising) strategy. You see, despite what you may think, no one knows who you are. No one knows about your business. Even if you have 10,000 people on your email list, I still argue that no one knows who you are because 10,000 people is nothing. And this is the way you need to be thinking all the time. If you think in this way, then you will always be on your toes, and always striving to come up with new and better ways to get the word out.

It also will keep you humble, and will encourage you to never give up on a strategy that works simply because your reputation has increased. If something works in bringing in new clients, by all means, keep doing that! Of course you need to remember that it is not all about you and your ego but coaching is a service about other people.

Does Anyone Care?

A corollary to the question, "Does anyone know about your business?" is "Does anyone care?" Again, the answer is a resounding, "NO!" Or at least, that's again how you need to be thinking if you want to expand your company. Asking this question— *does anyone care?*—over and over again helps to ensure that you stick with a PMA

Beware!
It doesn't matter how great of a coach you are. What matters is whether other people know and believe that you are a great coach. In other words, it is not just your talent that is going to make you famous and successful; it is the publicity, marketing, and advertising of that talent that is going to make you successful.

strategy that works, and ensures that you are evaluating your PMA strategy on a regular basis as you and your company continue to grow.

Really, Does Anyone Care?

The key to a solid PMA campaign is always asking yourself if what you are doing is truly worthy of note. Does anyone really care? Is it truly newsworthy? Would my clients *truly* care one iota if I did this? Would potential clients care? What about the press? My peers? My friends?

The reason I love this question so much—*does anyone care*—and also the previous one—*does anyone know about your business?*—is because if you honestly ask these two questions on a regular basis, it helps to put you in the right frame of mind for constant improvement. Despite Microsoft's success, undoubtedly there are still some people in the world who do not know who Bill Gates is, have never heard of Windows, and couldn't care less about the company and what it is doing. When you realize that, it helps to humble you as the head of your own small company, doesn't it? It helps you to realize that you are probably not doing all that you can to expand your sphere of influence as you may think. It helps you to develop new strategies for success, and to always question the status quo. It helps ensure you don't just rest on your laurels and become dry and stale. It helps keep you competitive.

Plan a Solid Publicity and Advertising Campaign

In the end, it really is your publicity, marketing, and advertising that are going to determine whether you progress beyond the "startup" phase. As mentioned before, a good PMA campaign can make up for nearly all other shortcomings. Therefore, it is in your best interest to take the time and energy—and find the discipline—to put together and implement a consistent and workable publicity, marketing, and advertising campaign.

While the three disciplines are certainly different, they are similar enough to wrap them all up into a single strategy. Basically, your publicity will be press coverage that you are not paying for; advertising is "press coverage" that you *are* paying for, and marketing is everything else, i.e., the big picture, how you answer the phone, what your website says, etc. The idea is to seamlessly integrate all three into a single profitable plan that brings in an endless supply of prospective clients. The plan must be

- written.
- do-able (it can't be "pie in the sky").
- easy enough that you can be consistent with it each week.
- as low-cost as possible.

Low-Cost Campaigns

This last part is key. Too many upstart entrepreneurs go overboard spending money, assuming optimistically that it's all going to come back to them in the short term in the form of an overflow of new business. I hope that happens for you, but the reality is usually far from that. A business takes time to establish itself in the minds of consumers, and requires discipline over time—not just a one-time splash of here today, gone tomorrow.

You see, if you spend too much up front, that's exactly what you are liable to see happen; you're here today, and gone tomorrow. It is said that 90 percent of upstart entrepreneurs close their doors after one year. One of the biggest reasons this happens is "Because we ran out of money." But that's not really why the business failed. The real reason is that the money they *did* have was not allocated efficiently.

Beware!
Money does not grow on trees. Think three times before you spend your limited funds on some "crucial" expense. Odds are, it really isn't that crucial.

Keep PMA Costs Really Low

More often than not, the biggest upstart entrepreneurial expense is the PMA budget. I urge you to do everything you can to keep that initial PMA budget as low as possible because if you don't, there are probably not going to be any expansion plans in the future!

So do everything you can to cut costs, and keep them low. If you think that you need a $200 weekly ad, see if you can figure out a way to get the same (or better) message across for $100 weekly, or better yet, $100 bi-weekly. Even better, wrack your brain to see if you can figure how to get the same amount of business by foregoing the print ad entirely, and instead using just referrals. Difficult, yes. Possible, absolutely.

Every Penny Counts

Of course, sometimes you just have to spend money, and sure, you're not going to figure out what works until you try. But from years of experience, I can tell you that in the long-run, you're going to be a whole lot happier, and whole lot more successful, if you become as frugal-minded as possible. Don't go out and buy fancy chairs and desks; don't go out and buy a full color ad; don't spend thousands on a website. Just don't do it. I guarantee you that it's all a waste of money. When you're running a business, especially a startup, every penny counts, and when we're talking expansion, even more so.

Your PMA costs need to stay as low as possible—now, tomorrow, and forever. Not only will this keep your overall expenses low, but it will actually result in a better PMA campaign—because instead of relying on your checkbook, you are forcing yourself to use your brain. The result is a more creative campaign, every single time.

I'm not going to go into the great details of publicity and advertising here in this book because there are so many other books—many listed in the appendix—that would do an even better job. My intent here is to instill within you the same fire for publicity, marketing, and advertising that I have within my heart, and inspire you to learn as much as you can about these various disciplines on an ongoing basis as you start and run your business.

If expansion is your goal, you simply cannot do it without good publicity, marketing, and advertising.

Wrap Up

Remember it is not just talent that makes the star; it is the publicity of that talent that makes the star. Too many entrepreneurs focus on being the best when what they should be focused on is being *known* as the best. There is a big difference between the two, and you'd be wise to think about it.

Expanding
Services Offered

The nice thing about being a coach (and there-fore an expert) is there are many spinoff disciplines into which you can expand.

The first, of course, is the publishing world. If you're a motivational coach, you need your own set of books—or even just one—to make you the expert.

Beyond that, you should consider getting onto the speaking circuit, whether it's speaking to college audiences, or corporate audiences, or even small private groups. You can put together small workshops and seminars that you produce yourself, or you can partner up with another company to do a joint event and thus share some of the responsibilities (and profits).

You can offer e-books, online workshops, and teleconferences that participants pay to be a part of, or you can offer them for free and use them as lead generation devices. Check out FreeConference.com for starters.

New and Different Directions

You can create subsidiary businesses within your company. For instance, I am working on opening a business bookstore as part of my business, Unstoppable Artists. While this would just be a new part of my current business, it itself would be technically run as a separate entity completely, and that means a whole new revenue stream.

You can also—like Robert Kiyosaki—create board games that relate to your subject matter. You can create films and audios that customers can watch at home, or listen to in their cars. You can propose a course at a local college or university. Having a Masters or PhD may be helpful, or even required, and this is precisely one of the reasons I went back to school for my masters, and am now enrolled in a PhD program. All of this will allow me to become an adjunct professor at many schools, and that's a wonderful credibility builder.

Don't Limit Yourself

Truly, you are only limited by your creativity. What started out for me as just a coaching firm in 2001 has morphed into a full-service business, marketing, and financial advisory firm today. And it is still in a state of positive change.

The sky is truly the limit as long as you're willing to think big, think outside of the norm, truly believe that nothing is impossible, and convince yourself that you're the one to prove it.

Hands-on vs. Hands-off

One very lucrative way to expand is to move from being a hands-on coach to becoming a hands-off coach. By this I mean that instead of working with clients one-on-one, you create products that can be used by multiple people simultaneously. As a result, you end up leveraging your time, which will ultimately result in more money.

For example, if you find yourself doing the same seminar over and over again, one idea might be to record it professionally, and then sell it for the same price online. Now you only have to do the in-person seminar if you want to, and in the meantime, you are making money while you sleep because the digital products are processed and delivered automatically using software.

Live Events

For some, doing live events is the true thrill. If you enjoy that, you can do what Dov Simens does at his Hollywood Film Institute. He offers his famous two-day film school in three different formats: A live course for those who want to be there in person, a DVD course for those who want to watch from home, or a web course offered directly online for those who want to watch immediately. As you might imagine, he does extremely well and makes an amazing living.

Other Possibilities

Other ways to create this leverage of time is to become hands-off by training and hiring additional coaches. While you may still choose to coach clients, you can make more money if other coaches are coaching their own set of clients as well.

We'll talk more about this later, but the key is to be sure to hire people who are as good (or better) than you. Also, you might consider raising your fees for more advanced clients, and offering lower rates for the less experienced coaches.

Don't Lose Touch

One very important thing to remember is that as you expand, you risk losing the personality associated with your smaller firm. As you expand, be sure that your customer service remains the same (or improves), and that you do not lose touch with why you became successful in the first place. For example, one coaching firm I know used to always make live sales calls. Now, they use a cheesy automated voice that leaves a message on my voice mail. It is clear that it is a recorded message and it's really tacky, and as a result I have lost a lot of trust in this coaching firm.

> **Beware!**
> Automation can be a good thing, but too much is a really bad thing. Everything in moderation.

In fact, one of my best clients said to me that the reason she chose my coaching firm above all others is because she could tell that I really cared about my clients, and that it was clear that she would receive true personal attention unique to her situation by working with me. Specifically she said that everyone else came across as too slick, whereas I came across as sincere. I have never forgotten that, and to this day, I make great efforts to remain grounded with my client base, even as my coaching firm expands.

Wrap Up

I hope it clear by now that my definition of expansion starts from day one. In fact, you may have gathered by reading this book that every aspect of running the company must be thought about and analyzed starting from day one—at least on the surface. The more you plan ahead, the less far behind you'll end up becoming. And planning ahead includes expansion. Whatever your intentions, it is important to know and understand where you business can go, and to prepare accordingly.

Even before you start your business, as part of your preparation, you should sit down with a piece of paper and create a timeline. Write down exactly where you see your business in ten years. Think about it. Ten years from now. Think big! Write down how many locations your business has, in which cities and countries, how many employees, etc. And then you have somewhere to go.

Expanding Into
New Markets

Once you get established in your home town or city, there will come a time when you seem to stop expanding. This is inevitable as every market has a saturation point, and eventually, you are going to have to branch out into other cities to continue to grow.

Therefore, your first step after profitability and market saturation is to start thinking about where else to go. Of course, you could (as the previous chapter mentioned) begin to offer additional products and services to the same client base. Or, you could take your current products and services and find new markets in which to sell them.

Going National

There are two ways to expand nationally. First, you can expand out in concentric circles from your homebase. For example, from a homebase in Manhattan, New York City, you would first expand to the other four boroughs, then to Westchester County, Connecticut, and New Jersey, and soon, the entire east coast, the mid-west, and finally the west coast.

Or you could expand by market size. For example, a show business-related firm based in New York would next want to expand to Los Angeles, then Chicago, and then Texas and Florida.

The trick with expanding nationally is that you need to be sure that what you're selling here is going to sell just as well there. Also, you need to be sure that the marketing that works here is going to work there. In some cases, you won't need to make any adjustments at all. In others, you will have to tweak everything, and in rare cases, completely overhaul the entire operation.

Determining Profitability

In each of these cases, you need to determine if it makes profitable sense to expand. You need to do a new break-even analysis for each new market, and also create a brand new PMA campaign strategy. You may—after conducting your analyses—determine that it doesn't make sense to expand at all. And that's a decision you should certainly try to figure out *before* you make the effort and expense of actually making the move.

In most cases, if you have a solid operations manual, the operation should translate nicely. That operations manual should act as a firm foundation to any national expansion plans. Think big guys! Remember that even McDonald's, Staples, and Morgan Stanley all started out with just one location back in the day. And so has Unstoppable Artists—which I eventually plan to expand to Los Angeles, Chicago, Florida, Vancouver, Toronto, London, Milan, Paris, Sydney, and Moscow. On that note, let's talk about your plans to go international.

Going International

Speaking of all those foreign cities, I'd be remiss if I didn't encourage you to think about taking your firm international once you establish yourself in your home country. Perhaps you're thinking that going international is going to be extremely difficult.

As we've already discussed, you can go national, and even international, without even leaving your home. It's really simple thanks to technology.

Instead of relocating to the new city, you simply work with clients and customers by phone, email, and now videoconference. I myself have never met many of my clients in person—simply because they live outside of my home market. Thanks to the internet, phones and Skype, getting an international expansion off the ground does not need to cost an arm and a leg, does not need to be all that complicated, and can start from the comfort of your very own home.

What about Physical Expansion?

Now, of course, as your business grows, you may decide that it actually makes sense for you to physically establish a presence in other cities. If so, the best way to prepare for this is to figure out which cities you might want to expand to now, long before the need actually arises.

One challenge of international expansion vs. national expansion is that once you cross the border, the laws change dramatically. Therefore, before you do expand (and this advice applies to a lot of things you do in business), be sure to consult with an attorney who is familiar with the laws of the branch country. The last thing you want to do is open up a foreign branch only to discover that you're operating in violation of a number of different laws and ordinances!

The most important thing to remember right now is that thanks to the internet, you can essentially be an international business without ever leaving your home country. I have many clients in other countries, but all of the business is conducted here in the United States. In other words, they pay me by credit card, and then our meetings are all by telephone. So even though I don't have locations in other countries yet, I still consider myself the CEO of an international company. This is the perfect way to start your international expansion.

Horizontal and Vertical Expansion

The idea of going deeper is also known as vertical expansion, i.e., you are staying within the same product/service area, but offering more and better of the same. In other words, once you have a solid coaching package in play, you might consider offering additional coaching packages. You might consider offering different price levels. You might experiment with different types of coaching, and to different types of clients.

For example, when I started out, my company was called Unstoppable Actors, and only offered motivational coaching. Then, I began to realize that by combining business coaching with the motivation, I had more to offer my clients. Soon, I added financial advising, and publicity services, and once I graduate from law school and pass the bar exam, I will also add legal counsel to the mix. Each of these additional value-added services is essentially an expansion, even though it may not seem that way at first glance.

Expanding Your Market Vertically

In addition, you can expand your market vertically as well. At first I was focused only on those actors who were seeking the motivation that they needed to continue. Then I realized I could also help up-and-comers as well, and began to market my services to those who already had a decent amount of success. My plan now is to expand even more vertically, to those who are already stars—in order to help them stay at the top. That is what going deeper is all about.

Again, the idea with any of this thinking is to constantly brainstorm ways to increase business, become more profitable, and help more people. I keep a pad of paper on my nightstand precisely because I am *always* thinking about how to expand things, and when inspiration strikes, I like to have a pad and paper handy to preserve those great ideas.

Expanding Your Market Horizontally

But going deeper is only half the battle; going wider is yet another expansion tactic you should consider. Also known as horizontal expansion, going wider focuses on offering the same (or different) products and services to a completely new client base. You are expanding your arms to welcome even more people in from your left and from your right.

For example, about a year after I started my own firm, I began to realize that people other than actors began coming to me asking for help. While I was promoting my business primarily to actors, I quickly found myself also coaching writers, directors, models, singers, inventors, athletes, and the like. Therefore, I changed the name from Unstoppable Actors to Unstoppable Artists—a perfect example of expanding horizontally within the same coaching field I had started out in.

Beware!

A big problem with a lot of upstarts is that they jump into horizontal expansion too soon. They start selling too much too soon to too many different markets without first establishing themselves vertically in one market. I recommend you focus on a single market, establish yourself, and then, once you are comfortably successful there, begin to expand horizontally.

Expanding What You Offer

You can also horizontally expand what you offer. Instead of just focusing on different coaching, you can offer books, project management, in-depth analyses. You can even start sister organizations that are related, but different, from your consulting firm.

For example, I started something called the American Break Diving Association, a networking group whose membership motto is "No Rules, No Excuses, No Regrets." While this concept is related to Unstoppable Artists, and the group is run as a subsidiary of Unstoppable Artists, it itself is its own business. The cross promotion between the different people in both groups is wonderful.

Perhaps the best example of a company going both deep and wide is Amazon.com. First, they went as deep as possible selling books. They continued to vertically expand by offering a better selection, better customer service, and working to reach as many book buyers as possible. Then, they began horizontally expanding into toys, electronics, kitchenware, etc. What Amazon did is a good model to follow; start with vertical expansion and once you are established, only then consider horizontal expansion.

▲

Wrap Up

Part of that expansion exercise from the last chapter overlaps with this one. Continue asking questions: Who are your customers? Where are they based? Where does your company do business? In how many countries? Which ones? Why? By when?

Start getting even more specific. Are you making $2,000 a month ten years from now, or $200,000 a month ten years from now? You absolutely *need* to be specific. It really does make a difference. Creating this ten-year strategy and writing it down is perhaps one of the best things you can do to help ensure the success of your efforts.

Hiring
and Firing

For most upstart businesses, the idea of being in such demand that you can't service everyone seems like a dream come true. In fact, this fallacy is so pervasive that most entrepreneurs don't plan for this incredibly awesome event, and as a result they crumble under the pressure.

You see, while it is undeniable that having a huge increase in demand can be the best thing that ever happens to a business, it can also be the worst. If you are not prepared to handle an influx of orders, a surge of clients, or a jump in popularity, then you risk forcing your enterprise into an unrecoverable downward spin. For example, if you receive an order for 100,000 units, but don't have the capacity to manufacture all of those units, you could end up with a very unsatisfied customer. If you suddenly receive requests from hundreds of people for your coaching services, but you don't have the time or manpower to deliver, you risk losing them all, and your reputation going south as a result. And that could spell the end of your entrepreneurial enthusiasm. Of course since coaching is different than selling cheeseburgers you may gain greater respect by being a very successful smaller business. Bigger isn't always better especially in a personalized service business.

Be Prepared for Success

So what to do? You need to approach success as you should everything in your business. Be prepared—for everything and anything. While many entrepreneurs instinctively prepare for the worst, very few seem to prepare for the best. You have to assume that your business very well may take off like a rocket. While the likelihood of that happening at the beginning of your entrepreneurial adventures is not very likely, it nonetheless is possible. And you need to be ready.

You need to prepare what I call a D.O.S., or (as I mentioned earlier) a demand overload strategy. Ask yourself these pertinent questions: Do I have the capacity to handle a doubling of business tomorrow? A tripling? If so, would the transition be seamless? If not, who do I need to keep in the wings to prepare for this demand overload? How much do I need to train them? Where do I *find* these people?

For instance, as a single motivational coach, you can only handle so much on your own. As a sole proprietor, you are wearing nearly every hat, from the actual coaching to the advertising and to the bookkeeping. For every hour you spend on bookkeeping or advertising, that's one less hour you can spend with a client. Therefore, as you grow, you might consider hiring an office assistant to handle some of the office tasks so you can focus more

Smart Tip
Your demand overload strategy should be a written part of your operations manual.

Tip...

on coaching. And when that demand exceeds your limits, you'll then need to hire additional coaches as well.

Hiring Coaches

Some people want to remain solo practitioners, so to speak, which is fine. Many coaches do very well on their own. If, however, you think you would like to expand one day then from day one, you should be thinking about the qualities you are going to require in additional coaches. A big mistake a lot of coaches make is assuming that they themselves are irreplaceable, and that no one can coach as well as they can.

Don't think this way! Once again, get your ego out of the way. If you think you're the one and only, then there's no way you are going to be able to expand. If you have additional coaches, it will not only allow you to expand, but it will also act as job security too. If you decide to take a vacation or you get sick, your other coaches would still be able to cover for you and keep the business afloat. Wouldn't that be nice? And don't you want to ensure that your company continues to help people long after you're gone?

You may decide that you never want to expand—and that is fine—but you would be remiss if you didn't plan for that situation nonetheless. The last thing you want is to suddenly find yourself in a position where you decide to change your mind, but unfortunately realize that you are not in a position to do what you want to do.

Know Enough to Hire and Fire

It is key that you think about hiring and firing additional staff from day one. And the only way you are going to know how to hire and fire people is by learning just enough about each of the jobs to be able to spot talent when you see it (so you hire the right people), and how to spot a slacker when you see it (so you fire the people who are slowing down the company).

The problem with many entrepreneurs is that they hire people precisely because they themselves "know nothing about that," and that's a mistake. Never—*never*—hire someone without knowing what it is that person actually does and how they do it. Of course, you don't have to be an expert in everything—and are not expected to be—but before you hire an accountant, you should certainly have a basic understanding of accounting and bookkeeping, and be able to do the basics yourself. Before you hire a marketing manager, you should certainly understand the basics of marketing theory. And before you hire a new coach to work with your clients, you should certainly know how to be a top-notch coach yourself. This all just makes sense when you think about it. How can you expect to hire a good employee if you don't know what you should be looking for in that candidate? By the same token, how can you know whether an employee is taking advantage of you, or not pulling his weight, if you yourself don't know what he should be doing. Study after study has shown that employees are less likely to take advantage of someone who knows the employee's specific job. So learn them all!

You Are the CEO

I know that statement seems like a tall order, but hey, an entrepreneur is most certainly not an employee. Unlike an employee, you are responsible for every single job in the business. You are responsible for marketing, advertising, publicity, networking, sales, customer service, fundraising, investing, accounting, bookkeeping, IT, human resources, strategy, vision, and the list goes on. You, my dear reader, are the CEO! The Chief Executive Officer!

And with that title comes big responsibility. You see, even with employees, you are still responsible for the decisions that each of those department heads make. If you don't know what each of them is doing or how they are doing it (at least to a reasonable extent), then shame on you.

To successfully expand your business (and to help you take some of the burden off of your shoulders, and help you run things more efficiently), you are going to *have* to hire additional help eventually. As with anything in an entrepreneurial venture, the sooner you start planning for this expansion, the better off you are going to be, and the more likely you will be able to jump on the opportunity should it present itself.

Hire Slowly, and Fire Quickly

Perhaps you've heard the famous adage: "Hire slowly, and fire quickly." The reason you want to hire slowly is that once you get someone on board who is a drag—well, it's a drag. Therefore, you should make every effort on the front end to hire the right person from the get-go. On the flip side, the reason you want to fire quickly is because as soon as you realize someone's a drag, you want to let them go quickly and immediately to avoid bringing the company down any further.

This, of course, is all a lot easier said than done. Often, when we need to hire, we're in a mad rush to do so, and we fail to interview and screen candidates as thoroughly as we should. And once you realize someone is not doing the job, it's often awkward and unsettling to have to fire that someone.

But fire we must, and hire the right people we must. It is well accepted that a company's employees are its most valuable assets. Therefore, it just makes logical sense to ensure that you only bring the right people on board. And it makes just as much sense to ensure that you quickly get rid of those who aren't the right fit.

The Benefit of Experience

From personal experience running four different businesses over the years, and from leadership positions in the Army and in Iraq, I can tell you that the initial hiring process may indeed involve you making a bunch of errors in judgment. That is to be expected because you may not know exactly what type of person you are looking for until you see them in action. When I initially brought additional coaches on board for Unstoppable Artists, I did not have a very big list of prerequisites, simply because I desperately wanted to expand. The result was that I brought on people who did not fit perfectly, and a lot of comments from clients revolved around the stark difference in experience and education between me and my coaches. I had more experience and education than all of them. I learned my lesson.

I eventually let my first group of coaches go and created a new profile for future coaches. It was important for me as a coach in the arts, that my coaches had experience in some aspect of show business as well as a masters Degree in some area of business. You will also want to make sure that they have, or are getting, some training in actually being a coach. You need to find people who are good listeners and have a knack for actually coaching other people. Remember, if they are just telling clients where to find auditions and which ones to go to, they are a consultants or advisors but not coaches.

In other words, I began to realize through my initial hiring process that my clients expected only the best of the best, and did not want those who are less experienced than I am to be their advisor.

Hire Slowly

In addition, I rarely will hire anyone these days without at least two interviews, if not three. Not only do the pre-interview levels of experience and education have to be met, but they must also go through more than one interview. I've discovered that you often don't really know if the person you met on day one is the real personality unless you schedule a second and third interview. If people present a consistently positive image by the third interview, they are probably who

Stat Fact
Most entrepre-
neurs hire too
quickly, and wait too long
before firing. Strive to break
free from this statistic.

they present themselves to be. You also need to check references and make sure the information they put on their resume or on your application is legit. Follow-up on your top candidates. You might even check their LinkedIn profiles or Facebook pages.

By taking things much more slowly, you ensure that you only bring people into your company who are up to the task. Moreover, the more slowly you hire, the less likely you are going to have to fire that person—and anything you can do that may help avoid that task will make you a much happier person.

But Fire Quickly

If you don't have the guts to fire people when it is clear that they are not a good fit, you are not only doing your company a disservice, but you are doing that person a disservice as well. You can't let them bring down your company, and you can't let them continue thinking they are doing a good job. Compassion is one thing, but lack of entrepreneurial discipline is something else entirely.

Sometimes you just have to let people go, and it sucks. And it's usually not much fun to have to fire someone. But the alternative is to cut off your nose to spite your face—you'll end up being the nice guy who ends up going down with a sinking ship.

This is why the adage insists you fire quickly. As soon as you diagnose a problem employee, and reasonable efforts to coach this person into compliance fail, *fire them!* Get rid of the dead weight as soon as possible. If they are not going to give you what you need, then you're foolish to keep them on board.

Make sure you fire for work reasons only. While you do not need to explain to someone why he or she is being let go, you should have it documented on file. Make sure to keep ongoing records of your staffs' work.

Interns and Work Study

Did I mention that it's often really hard to find the money to hire employees right off the bat, especially if you don't have a lot of startup capital? Don't fret! There really is a viable solution, and it is called interns and work study.

Instead of paying your employees in the form of a paycheck, you can instead pay them in the form of a learning experience and a mentor. For example, you can create a three-month intern program where each intern must agree to work for you for a minimum of 10–20 hours each week. In return, you offer them the opportunity to learn from you, either by working side by side with you, or by coaching them for a period of time each week at no charge. Or, you can use a combination of both.

The key to attracting top interns and work study employees (and regular employees for that matter) is to make sure that there is something in it for them. The more you can offer your people, the higher quality people you are going to entice into your business.

For instance, beyond free coaching, if you can offer connections, assistance, prestige, honor, or a multitude of other fringe benefits, the higher your intern talent pool will become. Along with Fringe benefits, you can demonstrate by your own coaching successes that they can learn from you and rise in the ranks as you have done. For example, being associated and training with Tony Robbins, you can be sure more doors will be opened for you down the road.

In addition, by offering free coaching and business advice to my interns, I give them even more than just experience. I help them lay the foundation for their own empire, and that is something you just can't put a price on. As a nice big bonus, my interns also get introduced to people in my circle of influence who they would just never meet otherwise.

What Can You Offer?

Think along these same lines: What can you offer your people that would make them want to intern with you? Believe it or not, you have a lot more to offer than you may realize, and often, it's the presentation that makes the difference. Don't sell the steak, as they say, sell the sizzle. By doing so, you help your potential interns to

Beware!
The more interns you bring on board, the more time it is actually going to require of you to manage your intern program. Don't forget that you are going to have to spend a fair amount of time showing and telling them what you want them to do.

realize that by working for you, they are getting the equivalent of a paycheck but in experience.

Also, realize that you don't need to have them every day. You can hire your first intern for just one day a week for four hours at a time. Then, if you hire four more, you can have a second hand to help you five days a week. That ends up being an additional 20 work hours a week that you just added to your total.

Try Before You Buy

The nice thing about bringing interns on board (and temporary help too, if you want to go through a temp agency) is that it's a very effective way to test the waters with them as potential employees in a non-committing environment. You may find that the best way to hire people is to first have them work as an intern or temp at low or no cost. By providing you with an extended hands-on interview over the course of a number of weeks or months, you are in a much better position to judge the work ethic and personality of each potential employee.

Where to find these interns? One place: the online bulletin boards. As of this printing, the best one is Craigslist. Where to find temps? Look in the yellow pages, or do a Google search.

The Fewer the Better...at First

Don't bring on so many people that they end up eating up all of your precious time. The fewer people you start out with, the better. I recommend two or three at most to get your feet wet. In terms of what to delegate, you can either cross train each of the interns so that they are all working on the same projects, or,

Beware!
Having interns takes a lot of work. Implemented properly, your intern program can truly help you expand. Managed improperly, it could drive your whole operation into a tailspin. Don't bring on five interns on day one.

you can assign a unique project to each of them. Both approaches are valid—your unique situation will help you determine which makes more sense in your company.

To help you in determining which method to use, you might want to keep in mind that eventually, most interns leave. You need to be prepared for their eventual departure. Therefore, for starters, you probably do not want to entrust interns with your most precious secrets, contacts, and projects. If they get knee deep into something and then suddenly disappear, you're going to be more stressed out than you ever were before. You need to create a system whereby each intern or intern project manager reports back to you at the end of every week with a written update on where everything currently stands, including contact numbers, appointments, meetings, progress, etc. If you create this type of system, it will help cushion the blow if that person suddenly bails out on you because you will have been kept in the loop each and every week.

Another solution is to use the cross-fertilization approach I mentioned above. In this case, no intern has lead on any one project, but rather, all of the interns collectively help out with all projects. This way, if someone leaves, you still have one or two who are still up to speed on what is going on. The downside is that there is no specialization, and it will require more of your time to organize this type of intern program.

The most important thing to remember from this chapter is that you should not limit your staff expansion simply because you feel you "don't have the money." As I always tell my clients, lack of money is *never* an excuse. Nor can it be for you. If you need additional manpower to expand and don't have the money—*no excuses. Figure it out.*

Wrap Up

Yes, hiring and firing staff can be a big hassle and drain. It should be a part of your mission to hire assistance and staff as soon as you choose to expand or find that you are being pulled in too many directions. Employees can help you grow upir business but at a cost, both literally and figuratively, Paying people means cutting into your profits and training people means cutting into your time. Even interns csn be draining you of valuable time spent coaching. So make sure you are ready before you start hiring people. Don't just do it because you think it makes you look more prestigious.

Hiring an
Office Manager

Ahhh, the big day has come where you can't handle everything yourself anymore! Yes, this day will come, and this is the day when you are going to find yourself in need of an office manager and/or personal assistant. The reason I combine the two positions together is that you may decide you need more help with your personal life as well to help free up the time you need to run the company.

Either way, there will come a time when you are going to want to get a right-hand person—someone who helps you stay on track, stay organized, and run the company. A vice president of sorts.

Hire the Best

As you might surmise, this person is a very important hire, and one that should not be made rashly, abruptly, or without serious deliberation. This person will be the one whose presence allows you to take a one-week vacation without worrying whether the business will survive. This person will help you organize and manage all of your various projects—and at this point, those will be book projects, speaking events, other companies perhaps, and the list goes on. Eventually, you are just not going to be able to do it all on your own anymore, and you're going to have to relinquish some of the total authority you have become accustomed to from the very first day you opened up shop.

Learning to Let Go

Now, you have to start letting go. You have to start trusting others to help you run your company as well, if not better, than you did going solo. This is precisely why this person—whomever you choose—must be a really special person. You need to be sure that they are going to be capable of multitasking just as efficiently as you have been doing up to that point. You need to be sure they understand where the business is going, and can grow with it. You need to be sure that they hold the very same vision as you do.

This is not just another employee who can be easily replaced. The idea here is to find someone who can grow with you. Of course, not everyone will stay with you forever, but you should seek to find someone who is going to stay with your company for at least a reasonable amount of time after they learn the ropes—for it will be somewhat of a hassle to retrain a new office manager or personal assistant if the first one leaves.

Beware!
You need to pay your office manager/personal assistant. This is a time-intensive position with a lot of responsibility. To ask someone to do this voluntarily is asking a lot, no matter how much experience you may be providing this person.

Trust Them with Your Life

Once you do find the right person, and hire that person, you've got to realize that this person is now responsible for a very large portion of your success. If this person fails in their duties, takes advantage of you, or worse, your business could suffer immeasurably.

For this reason, while you of course want to let this person do what you hired him to do, you also want to ensure that you are keeping an eye on him. The whole idea of an office manager, though, is someone you can trust to work independently to get things done (in order to free up your own time so you can get even more important things done). But that doesn't mean you should just assign this person the position, and leave him to his devices. You have to keep an eye on him; let him know he is being watched.

It is well accepted that if employees *know* that the owner of a retail store actually watches the security tapes from the sales floor, they are less likely to steal. Employees need to know that they are being watched. When they know this, their behavior is always more positive.

Move the Company Forward

The reasons for keeping an eye on your office manager/personal assistant go beyond just avoiding theft—you're also checking to make sure that this person is driving your company down the right path. This of course goes for all of your employees, but particularly the person who is helping you run the entire operation. You want to have regular meetings with this person to ensure that both of you are always and forever on the same page, thinking alike, and moving towards the same goal. If so, then this person is going to help make your life a whole lot easier, and your bank account a whole lot wealthier. If not, trouble.

Plan for the Worst

Just as with interns, a word of caution, and even more seriously noted. This person—unlike an intern—is essentially running your *entire* business. If this person leaves and you are not prepared, you are more than inconvenienced. If this person leaves and you are not prepared, you are stranded.

Therefore, you need to set things up so that if your office manager/personal assistant suddenly leaves, you don't drown. You can help avoid this company meltdown by ensuring your office assistant/personal assistant brings you fully up to speed at the end of every week through a written report, or at the very least, an oral report. You should also share all files so you can access everything if he or she leaves.

Smart Tip

Tip...

There are a lot of great books on how to be a good manager, how to deal with problem employees, etc. It would benefit you to read them.

Remember, the mark of a good entrepreneur is one who plans ahead, for both successful events *and* unfortunate events. You have to plan for the unfortunate situation when your people leave you. Do not be caught unprepared! Think it all out ahead of time. Think of all the ways you could alleviate the problems if someone were to leave, especially your office manager/personal assistant long before they leave.

Three Bits of Advice

First, your company operations manual is key. That needs to be fully updated with every task, duty, and responsibility of the position.

Next, you might think about cross-training someone else to act as a backup to your office manager. No Broadway show goes up without understudies and swings who can jump in and take over if someone doesn't show. Your business is no different. Think about who could jump in if ever the main player has to leave.

Third, and this is perhaps the best advice, you should strive to avoid that person wanting to leave in the first place. Compensate him fairly, treat him with respect, provide challenging work, and create a positive work environment and you may in fact never have to experience such an upheaval. Of course people leave for all sorts of personal reasons so no matter how well you treat employees, be prepared.

Just Trust Them

That all being said, in the end, you just have to trust that the people you hire are the right people for the job and are going to stick around for the long haul. You are hiring someone to help make your life easier and help your business run more smoothly. If after you hire this person you are constantly wondering what he is doing and if he can be trusted—and of course, this applies to all employees—then you're just transferring the stress from one area of the business to another.

You hired this person to help relax the situation, right? Then trust him!

Trust but Verify

There's an expression, "Trust but verify." This is how you need to proceed in this situation. You have to trust that you hired someone who is trustworthy and responsible and dependable, and at the same time, take the time to verify that they continue to be trustworthy, responsible, and dependable. There's a finesse to doing this properly—the last thing you want to do is make your employees think you are always checking up on them. Hence, this is exactly why establishing a clear and simple reporting system is very useful.

It is said that the best followers are those who provide status updates without having to first be asked. Well, that's the type of employees you want; those who regularly volunteer information and status reports, rather than the types who hoard their information and force the boss to pry information out of them. Talk about a drag and a waste of time! You want to make it clear from the get-go that you expect regular reports from your employees, and that you specifically do not want to have to constantly keep tabs on them.

Nonetheless, there's another expression that is also appropriate: "Keeping an honest person honest." That's exactly how you should manage your office manager, coaches, and other employees. Ideally, you will have hired honest people to begin with (did you do your background checks?) and your instincts will have been spot-on correct. You should still keep an eye on them, but a casual eye. If you hired correctly, and if your operations manual is well written, you should ideally be able to just relax and let your employees do their job.

Outline for them exactly what their responsibilities are, let them know that you expect progress reports on a regular basis, be sure to set up frequent meetings, and that being said—just let them loose. They'll do just fine.

Beware!
Hiring those first employees is sometimes difficult for a solo entrepreneur because of control issues. While it's sometimes hard to delegate, you must learn to do so without micromanaging if you want to successfully expand.

Wrap Up

You may think that expansion is the last thing on your mind, and that these sections are completely inapplicable to you. "I just want to start and run a small business," you might say. In reply, I'd say, "Do you not realize that growing from no clients to your first clients is itself an expansion?" All you are doing is planning—contingency planning. You are planning for any and all possibilities, because that is what a good entrepreneur does.

21

Selling
It

I'd be a big liar if I told you that running an entrepreneurial enterprise is an easy thing to do. No, the truth is that
it's actually one big pain in the butt. Sure, it's fun, and exhilarat-
ing, but it also comes with a price—the price that comes with
being the head of a company, rather than simply an employee

who gets to go home at 5 P.M. and forget about everything until the next morning. That just is not the case when running your own company.

Starting the business, and getting it to the point where you are actually making a profit on a consistent basis is a great thing indeed. However, it is going to take a whole lot of work and involve a whole lot of heartache along the way to get it to a point of truly feeling that you are established. Even then, it still takes a whole lot of effort to keep an entrepreneurial firm operating efficiently.

For that reason, there may indeed come a time when you decide that you would like to do something else. This might—key word: *might*—be a perfect time to sell the company. There are a few questions that you might want to ask yourself at this point to determine if selling is the right thing to do.

Deciding to Sell

First, is selling it really what you want? If you sell it, you are removing yourself almost completely from the business and may not ever be able to re-associate yourself with it. You will also probably lose all the income associated with it, unless you structure a sales deal whereby you retain residual income. While the main idea of selling a business is to cash out and make a huge sum of money on the sale, there's a price that you pay for selling, and you need to be aware of that.

Second, if you sell it, you need to know exactly what you plan to do with the money you receive from that sale. Any entrepreneur who sells his business without a clear plan for investment of that money is missing a crucial step. If you don't have a plan for where you intend to spend that money, you risk squandering it before you even know it is gone. If you cash out your business, ideally you want to make sure that the money you gain from the sale is re-invested at the same or higher rate of return elsewhere.

But if you decide that you do want to sell, that's only half the battle. You still need to find a buyer.

Who Will Buy?

Many entrepreneurs dream of starting a business to help them fulfill their dream of freedom from a job in the first place. And many entrepreneurs rudely discover that starting a sole proprietorship does not free you from a job; it just changes who your boss is, and requires that you work even longer hours than you did at your regular job.

Smart Tip

Tip...

You can't value the business yourself. It's a good idea to bring in an independent valuator.

Therefore, selling the business after you have established it may very well be the first time that you receive that freedom that you so desperately sought when you started your business. And if indeed you do want to sell the business, you need to realize that you need more than a desirous seller (you), you also need an eager buyer. And therein lies the rub. Just because you want to sell your business and move to the Caribbean doesn't mean that someone else is necessarily going to want to buy it.

Valuing Your Business

It's simply a matter of supply and demand. What is going to make your company in demand involves (among other things):

- what the profit margin is
- what is unique about the company
- how well the company can be run without you, and
- whether the client base is loyal to you, or to the company as a whole.

We'll go into each of these briefly in the next section.

The Profit Margin

There are many ways to professionally value a business, but the informal process I present here is enough to give you a fair idea of the various factors that buyers look for when making their decision whether to buy.

Determining the profit margin is easy. Figure out how much money is left over after all expenses are paid each month. If it's a large amount, the profit margin is high, and the higher the demand for the business is going to be. Often, a professional valuator will use an earnings and profit multiplier over a period of four to six years to determine how much the business is worth. As a result, with a higher demand that comes from the higher profit margin comes a higher price that you can legitimately ask for the business.

Uniqueness

Whether the company is unique is a little trickier to determine. You have to look at all the other competitors in your industry and, as impartially as possible, determine if your company is truly different from them all. Beyond that, is the originality a competitive advantage, or is it negligible? In some cases, the fact that there is a difference between your business model and the competition's is actually a detractor. In most cases, though, the more unique a company is, the more you can ask for it. And if you happen to have intellectual property (patents, trademarks, trade secrets, etc.) that is unmistakably associated with your company, then that assures your uniqueness, and can really help to boost your company's sale value.

Independent Systems

The next question is whether a new CEO can profitably run the company without you on board. The answer to this question is found in your company operations manual. If you have created a good one, then buyers will certainly feel more comfortable buying the business. They will take a look at the operation manual, and—if you did a good job preparing it (and assuming it is an accurate reflection of the business)—they will realize that you set up your company in such a standardized manner that it can translate easily to the new owners. Only if they feel comfortable running the business without you will a potential buyer feel confident in buying the business.

Client Loyalty

Finally, a huge issue is whether the current clients are loyal to the company as a whole, or just to you. If the latter, then when you leave, so will all of the clients, and then the buyers will be stuck with a mere skeleton of a business. Many businesses have failed after the owner left because the clients were not fans of the business as much as they were a fan of the personality that ran the business. For this reason, it is often recommended that the old owner remain on staff for a crossover period with the new owners to allow the clients to gain familiarity with the new owners. However, sometimes this even is not enough, so the more you can ensure that the owners are buying a business, and not a frame, the more likely you are to sell the business, and at a fair price.

Of course, once again it is important to factor into the equation that you are not selling widgets or cheeseburgers but actually a service that helps people. You, therefore, have to consider the need to sell to someone who has adequate credentials as a coach since you should have a moral and ethical responsibility to your clients.

Finding a Buyer

Assuming your business fits the typical mold of a sellable enterprise, the next step is to actually find a buyer. Here, it's simply a matter of marketing and publicity.

First, you can search online and find a business broker—someone who exclusively focuses on helping entrepreneurs sell their business. More independently, you can post a listing on Craigslist and other online forums. You can also take an advertisement out in a newspaper letting people know that you are seeking a buyer. Certainly, mentioning that you are seeking a buyer on the homepage of your company website might help you find someone. Heck, maybe a prospective client ends up being that special someone who eventually purchases the business.

Wrap Up

The key to finding a buyer (for your business and for your services in general) is that you just have to keep blabbing to everyone that you meet. Tell everyone. This same principle applies to gaining clients too. The more you talk, the more others will talk, and eventually, word will spread and you'll eventually start receiving phone calls and emails from people who are interested. Just make sure that whomever you decide to sell to knows what heor she is doing. You'll never forgive yourself if a year after you sell, the company goes under because you sold to someone who couldn't handle it. When a business is service oriented (such as selling an accounting practice of a dental practice) you need to make sure the buyer has the credentials to handle it. Therefore, you need someone with an understanding of coaching and not just someone with a business degree.

Franchising It

Let's say that you decide that you don't want to sell. Instead, you want to expand even more. And let's say that you have the most standardized operations manual on the planet. If so, then you might want to consider franchising your business.

▲

Absolutely the most important consideration is whether you have a franchisable business model. In other words, is it easily copyable? Is the concept developed down to a science that can be easily implemented by another owner far away from the home office? Can a quality control system be implemented to ensure that the service a client receives from a franchise in Florida is the same as from a franchise in Ohio? If the answers to these questions are yes, then you might consider franchising.

The big question, though, is why would you want to?

Pros and Cons of Franchising

There are certainly a number of benefits to becoming the owner of a franchised business concept. The first reason is that you can make a whole lot of money. In accordance with standard franchise protocol, each new franchisee typically pays a large lump sum—anywhere from $20,000 to as high as millions of dollars—to the home office for the privilege of opening their franchise. Basically, what they are paying for is the right to use a trademarked (and valuable) company logo and business model. In return, the home office puts up all of the upfront costs for the new location, which relieves the new franchisee of that difficult burden.

Then, from that point forward, the owner of the franchise would receive a percentage of the franchisee's sales, and in return, would be in charge of spearheading a company-wide advertising campaign on behalf of all the franchisees. The nice thing for the home office is that the money for the advertising campaign doesn't come from the home office—it is paid for by all of the various franchisees. Are you beginning to see how you could make a lot of money with a franchise?

Job Change

Beyond the financial benefits, running a franchise changes your job description from manager/supervisor to trainer/supervisor. For some, this may be a preferable position. Instead of managing the entire operation of the various satellite locations of your coaching business, you let the franchisees handle all that. As a franchise home office, your primary focus would

Tip...

Smart Tip

Look for service franchises and contact some owners. You need to speak with people in similar types of businesses.

now be on preparing training programs for the franchisees, and supervising the quality control of each franchise.

On the flip side, by franchising your business concept you give up some control, because each franchisee owns their own franchise. You do not own their locations, and there are certain rules you must now abide by when working with your franchisees. You see, your franchisees are accountable to you, but they are not owned by you. And that's a big consideration.

However, can you imagine if every McDonald's restaurant around the world were owned by the home office? I myself just find it very hard to see them running every one of their 31,000-plus restaurants efficiently if they were all run by managers instead of owners. The owners take a much greater pride in their restaurants precisely because they own them, whereas a manager is merely an employee and will not work as hard to ensure quality control.

While running a franchise could make things easier for you, it can, however, also make things a lot more difficult too. For instance, there can be a lot of new legal paperwork that you would now be responsible for, and you would now have to abide by many new regulations under the franchising rules which may cramp your style and take some of the "fun" out of being the head honcho. While going the franchise route is definitely the way to go for many services businesses, it's ultimately a decision that you are going to have to make only after careful deliberation.

How to Find Your First Franchisee

If you do decide that going the franchise route is the way to go, and that your business is indeed franchisable, the next step would be to file the appropriate paperwork with the local and national authorities, and to that end, you might want to speak with a franchise attorney.

Next, it's sales time. You need to set up a website, advertise the opportunity, distribute brochures, etc. You might want to consider taking an ad out in *Entrepreneur Magazine*—their classified section in the is back reserved almost exclusively for those selling franchise opportunities.

And then, of course, you have to interview and qualify those who show interest. The most important criteria is whether these prospects have the funds necessary to purchase their franchise. Without those funds, it doesn't matter how qualified they may be otherwise.

The requirement for the upfront money cost is one of the reasons why franchises are usually more successful than traditional entrepreneurial startups. If the franchisee was able to find this large amount of investment money in the first place, it is clear that *someone* trusted him enough to do so, or that they were able to raise money successfully on their own. That alone says a lot about someone.

In addition, given all the money franchisees are paying upfront, they are expecting that they are going to receive a truly branded company that people have heard of, and that they are going to receive extensive training, support, and guidance from day one. So don't think that the franchise model is just an easy way to get money from people. In the end, you still have a lot to deliver to your individual franchise owners.

Wrap Up

Remember that you are expanding from day one. Right now, franchising may be the last thing from your mind, but what if in a few years, it is the most logical solution? The only way to know is to constantly look at your business with expansionary eyes from day one, and keep a finger on the pulse of your entire operation every step of the way. My best advice is to run your business under the assumption that you are going to franchise it one day. At the very best, you'll be ready. At worst, you'll have one of the most organized and structured businesses in town.

There are some franchised coaching businesses, such as The Growth Coach and Action Coach. One place to research coaching franchises is at www.Franchise direct.com where you will find business service franchises. The key to opening a coaching franchise is having a coaching system or modality that can be easily taught and has been proven effective.

23

Keeping
It

Of course, you might decide that you don't want to sell your coaching firm, and that you just want to keep your business as it is. Maybe you are completely happy with the way things currently are. If so, you may decide that you want to continue to run it as a source of income for the foreseeable future. That's great!

You just need to remember one important thing: Your sustenance depends on whether the business continues to do well. If you keep it, you need to continue to work on it constantly, developing it, refining it, and ensuring that it stays current and up-to-date with the times and with the competition.

Smart Tip

Tip...

You might want to consider creating your own TV, or radio show. That will help you on the path to millions a lot more quickly.

Of course, if you're a savvy financier in addition to being a savvy entrepreneur, you will be sure to pay yourself first from each paycheck, and then re-invest that money into other enterprises to help hedge against the business. Ideally, your coaching business should not be your only source of income. Multiple streams of income is the name of the game, and the sooner you get these multiple streams flowing into your bank account, the more at ease you will ultimately be. One of those streams could come from your book royalties; another stream from your speaking appearances.

Become Savvy

It is said that most people who are rich today got that way by first starting their own business, and then second, by investing their profits from that business into both the stock market and real estate. This is a famous model to follow with a long history of success to back it up. You could do worse things with your money.

I recommend that while you are actively learning how to make money from your business, you also take the time to learn how to profitably invest in both the stock market and real estate. It is a proven fact that most people who win the lottery end up in debt one year later. They get their millions of dollars in winnings, and because they never took the time to learn about money, they squander their winnings and find themselves poor twelve months later.

Your coaching business could very well be your own personal lottery ticket. While the vast majority of coaches are not millionaires, some of them—Tony Robbins and Robert Kiyosaki for instance—certainly are. And yes, I honestly believe that you can become the next Tony Robbins or Robert Kiyosaki. There is no reason why you can't make millions as a coach, and then invest all that money into stocks and real estate. Sounds like a perfect plan to me.

Deciding When Enough Is Enough

At every step of your entrepreneurial journey, you should ask yourself, "Is this enough?" There is no reason to continue pushing forward with expansion and hiring and growth if you've already reached your goal and you're happy. In fact, if you get to a point where you don't want to expand anymore—congratulations! You've done it!

I do not say this to discourage you from expanding to your heart's content. I say this because the last thing I want you to do is get so completely lost in your business that you lose sight of other things that may also be important—like friends, family, vacations, and heck, maybe even other business endeavors. It's quite possible that this coaching business becomes just a stepping stone to an even more profitable business, and that's why I talk about selling it, franchising it, etc. It's happened with others, and it can happen to you.

Know When to Stop

There is in fact a point beyond which you shouldn't take your business. Growth at any cost is not a smart strategy. For every business the breaking point is different, and only you are in a position to judge. But be aware that many otherwise successful businesses went down the tubes when they pushed forward beyond what was best for them, their company, and their clients. Arthur Anderson is a perfect example; their greed and ambition pushed the company's original mission right out the door, and forced the company to close its doors forever.

You can help avoid a similarly disastrous fate by regularly consulting with peers, friends, and advisors along the way as you grow. Often, an impartial third party is in the best position to give you the best advice on where to expand and whether you even should expand. In the end, though, you have just got to go with your heart and always be on alert that there indeed is a limit to how far you can (or should) go with every particular business, and you tread beyond that point at great risk.

Dollar Stretcher

The more you learn about how to profitably invest money, the more you are going to be able to stretch your dollars. Take the time to learn.

Beware! Expansion sometimes is not the best strategy for you to take. For some businesses, expansion was the final nail in the coffin.

Ensuring Generational Longevity

If you do decide that you want to keep your company and never want to sell, at the very least, you should figure out what you want to happen to the company when you die. By that time, you certainly will have helped thousands of people, and quite a few would be very disappointed to discover that you just let the business die with along you.

For this reason, you will want to make sure that you plan ahead. At the very least, update your last will and testament with instructions on who should take over the company when you pass on. Better yet, start grooming your successors long before you think you'll need them. Better safe than sorry.

Remember that while your successor can be someone from your family, it surely doesn't have to be, and in some cases, shouldn't be. This is all something you will want to discuss with your family, friends, and other advisors, to help put together a plan to ensure that the business—and your legend—lives on long after you pass. You've put all this work into creating this business; it just makes sense to take that little bit of additional time and effort to ensure that your business continues to help other people long into the future.

While you yourself may not live beyond a hundred, your business certainly can. Your business can be the mark you make on history that forever secures you a place in the history books.

Wrap Up

Perhaps in the end, you'll decide you want to keep your company as it is. That's fine, and that's great! Part of the allure of starting a business is to enjoy the pride of ownership. Truly, just knowing that your income is coming from something that you created from the ground up, and that you have a company that runs cleanly, efficiently, and profitably is something all entrepreneurs can be proud of.

Expect
the Best

Often when I read a how-to book, the author will use others who are successful in the field as a way to show you what is possible, but in their effort to do so, inadvertently insult the reader. For example, I'll come across something like this: "While you can't expect to be as great as Tiger

Woods . . ." or, "Although you are probably not going to become the next Tony Robbins . . ."

No! No! No! This negativity is anathema to me! As far as I am concerned, you *can* expect to be as great as Tiger Woods. And yes, I *do* believe that you can become the next Tony Robbins or the next Robert Kiyosaki. In fact, I really hope so! I am rooting for you 100 percent!

Succeeding as an entrepreneur is difficult enough, and especially difficult in such a demanding field as motivational coaching; the last thing you need is me telling you that you're probably not going to be successful. That is just plain mean and insulting.

Hey, I hope you *do* become the next Tony Robbins. That means this book helped you to become one of the most well-known, respected, and called upon motivational coaches and speakers in the world. And that would make me very proud indeed.

Mario Andretti once said, "If you feel like you're in control, then you're not driving fast enough." He is 100 percent correct. Don't strive to be in control; strive to be better than the competition. If you feel like you're in control, first off, you are probably just deluding yourself, and more importantly, it means you are not taking enough chances. The successful entrepreneurs are not those who are in control; they are the ones who are constantly trying to push the envelope.

On that note, meet you at the top (and in the winner's circle).

Appendix
Coaching Resources

When I say you need to read all of these books, I truly mean it. Go to Amazon.com or BN.com and order every single one of these books. They should all be permanent additions to your library, and they should each be read with a pen and highlighter for you to mark up with notes and ideas. If you buy and read each of the books below and act on their wisdom (in conjunction with the book you are holding in your hands), your new coaching business will be well on its way to success.

Suggested Reading

The Anatomy of Buzz: How to Create Word of Mouth Marketing, Emanuel Rosen, New York: Currency/Doubleday, 2002

The 48 Laws of Power, Robert Greene, New York: Penguin Books, 2000

Anthem, Ayn Rand, Caldwell, Idaho: Caxton Printers, Ltd.,1946

Battle Cries for the Underdog: Fightin' Words for an Extraordinary Life, Volume I, Monroe Mann, AuthorHouse, 2006

Brag: The Art of Tooting Your Own Horn Without Blowing It, Peggy Klaus, New York: Business Plus/Grand Central Publishing/Hachette Book Group, 2004

Building a Financial Services Clientel: A Guide to the One Card System, O. Alfred Granum, Barry Alberstein, and Delia Alberstein, Cincinnati, OH: National Underwriter Company, 2001

The Cashflow Quadrant: Rich Dad's Guide to Financial Freedom, Robert T. Kiyosaki with Sharon L. Lechter, New York: Warner Books, 2000.

Closing Techniques (That Really Work!) Stephan Schiffman, Cincinnati, OH: Adams Media Corporation, 2004

Cold Calling Techniques (That Really Work!), Stephan Schiffman, Cincinnati, OH: Adams Media Corporation, 2007

Customer Satisfaction Is Worthless; Customer Loyalty Is Priceless. How to Make Them Love You, Keep You Coming Back, and Tell Everyone They Know, Jeffrey Gitomer, Austin, TX: Bard Press, 1998

E-Myth Mastery: The Seven Essential Disciplines for Building a World Class Company, Michael Gerber, New York: HarperCollins Publishers, 2005

Full Frontal PR: Building Buzz about Your Business, Your Product, or You, Richard Laermer, New York: Bloomberg Press, 2004

Getting Started in Personal and Executive Coaching, Stephen G. Fairley and Chris E. Stout, New York: John Wiley & Sons, 2003

Guerrilla Marketing: Easy and Inexpensive Strategies for Making Big Profits from Your Small Business, Jay Conrad Levinson with Jeannie Levinson and Amy Levinson, Boston: Houghton Mifflin, 2007

Guerrilla Marketing in 30 Days, Jay Conrad Levinson and Al Lautensalger, Irvine, CA: Entrepreneur Press, 2005

Guerrilla Networking: A Proven Battle Plan to Attract the Very People You Want to Meet Jay Conrad Levinson and Monroe Mann, Garden City, NY: Morgan James Publishing, 2007

How to Advertise, Kenneth Roman, Jane Maas, and Martin Nisenholtz, New York: Thomas Dunne Books/St. Martin's Press, 2003

How to Position Yourself as the Obvious Expert: Turbocharge Your Consulting or Coaching Business Now, Elsom Eldridge and Mark Eldridge, Warren, MI: Mastermind Publishing, 2004

The Luck Factor: Changing Your Luck, Changing Your Life, The Four Essential Principles, Dr. Richard Wiseman, New York: Hyperion, 2003

Mastering Online Marketing, Mitch Meyerson and Mary Eule Scarborough, Irvine, CA: Entrepreneur Press, 2007

Multiple Streams of Income, Robert G. Allen, Hoboken, N.J.: John Wiley & Sons, 2004

Rich Dad's Before You Quit Your Job: 10 Real-Life Lessons Every Entrepreneur Should Know about Building a Multimillion-Dollar Business. Robert Kiyosaki and Sharon Lechter, New York: Business Plus/Grand Central Publishing/Hachette Book Group, 2005

Rich Dad, Poor Dad: What the Rich Teach Their Kids about Money—That the Poor and Middle Class Do Not!, Robert T. Kiyosaki with Sharon L. Lechter, New York: Time Warner, 1998.

Startup: Start Your Own Consulting Business, Entrepreneur Press and Eileen Figure Sandlin, Irvine, CA: Entrepreneur Press, 2001

Startup: Start Your Own e-Business. Entrepreneur Press, Robert McGarvey and Melissa Campanelli, Irvine, CA: Entrepreneur Press, 2005

Tools and Techniques of Financial Planning by Stephan R. Leimberg, Martin J. Satinsky Robert J. Doyle, Jr, Michael S. Jackson, Cincinnati, OH: National Underwriter Company, 2007

The Theatrical Juggernaut—The Psyche of the Star, Monroe Mann, AuthorHouse, 2006

The Ultimate Guide to Google AdWords, Perry Marshall and Bryan Todd, Irvine CA: Entrepreneur Press, 2006

What Rich People Know (and Desperately Want to Keep Secret), Brian Sher, New York: Macmillan Publishers, 1999

Your Marketing Sucks, Mark Stevens, New York: Three Rivers Press/Random House, 2005

Websites

Legal Sites

www.BizFilings.com

www.Incorporate.com

www.LegalZoom.com

www.Nolo.com

Coaching Firms and Training

www.CTI.com

www.NLP.com

www.TobyRobbins.com

www.CoachingFederation.org

www.Icoachingacademy.com

www.NLPcoaching.com

www.Resultscoaches.com

www.Unstoppableartists.com

www.DavidEllzey.com

www.Lifecoachaustin.com

Website Domain Companies

www.BlueHost.com

www.GoDaddy.com

www.Hostgator.com

Email List/Website Companies

www.iContact.com

www.EasyWebAutomation.com

www.iBuilt.net

www.ArtBrownArt.biz

Credit Card Processing Companies

www.PayPal.com

www.Intellipay.com

www.Checkout.Google.com

About
the Authors

RICH MINTZER is a business writer who has written a number of successful books about starting a wide range of businesses. He is also a ghostwriter who runs a ghostwriting service called Your Book Your Way.

MONROE MANN, F.O.W., is the founder of Unstoppable Artists, a business coaching firm, publicity agency, and management firm for artists whose clients have appeared in/on *Ellen, Good Morning America, Inside Edition, Dr. Keith, ABC News, FOX News, The Boston Globe, Hollywood Reporter, Backstage, The New York Times, The New York Post, Glamour, Variety, TimeOut NY, San Francisco Chronicle, LA Times, Orlando Sentinel,* and the list goes on and on. He is a graduate of Franklin College in Lugano, Switzerland, where he studied international economics and French. He holds a Masters of Entrepreneurship from Western Carolina University, and is working towards his JD/MBA through Pace Law School and Lubin School of Business, and his Certified Financial Planner credentials through Boston Institute of Finance.

Monroe is also the founder of Loco Dawn Films, LLC; a union actor; the lead singer of the band, Running for Famous; the director, writer, and co-star of *Origami Deathmatch*, *In the Wake*, and *Hollywood Combat*, and is the author of a number of books including *The Theatrical Juggernaut*, *To Benning and Back*, *Battle Cries for the Underdog*, and *Guerrilla Networking* (with Jay Conrad Levinson). For more information, visit Unstoppable Artists. com.

Glossary

60/40 rule: once you get your first client, you need to spend 60 percent of your marketing time devoted to *keeping* that first client, and the remaining 40 percent of your marketing time trying to snag new clients. Remember that it is always easier to keep a current client than it is to sell a new one.

Accountability: the only way to ensure that you won't quit and give up. In other words, the more people who know about your big plans and projects, the less likely you are to give up on them.

Accounting: what you need to learn how to do like a pro if you want to ensure the continued success of your business. Without understanding accounting, you frankly have no idea whether your business is doing well or doing poorly, and you can't just go on a hunch.

Balance sheet: a record of the total assets and total liabilities for your business at a specific period of time, usually created at the end of every month. The balance sheet from each current month must always be compared with previous months to determine trends and help diagnose problems.

Bootstrapping: when someone starts a business from scratch with no money and no infrastructure—on a wing and a prayer.

Buy-in: whether someone trusts you enough to spend their hard-earned money on you and your services. The more you can get your clients to trust you, the better.

Buzz: what happens when you are the talk of the town, and everyone wants to work with you. The idea is to spread the word about you and your company *everywhere*.

CCC: Cost, Credibility, and Control—the differences between advertising and publicity. Advertising costs money, has low credibility, but gives you high control. On the other hand, publicity is low cost, affords high credibility, but gives you little control.

Client: the most important person in the world to the success of your business.

Coach: in the self-help context, someone who pushes another individual or group to work harder and smarter by asking the right *questions*, as opposed to providing answers.

Coaching packages: the best way to sell your services, because you get a larger commitment from the client, and that means less sales effort in the future.

Coaching skills: the body of tools you use when working with your clients one on one. The more skillful you are at coaching, the better you are going to be able to service your clients by helping them get past obstacles and reach their goals.

Consultant: generally someone giving advice who proclaims to be or is known to be an expert. Someone who gives *answers*, as opposed to someone who asks questions.

Expenses: what you need to keep *as low as possible* (and then even lower). You want to try and minimize expenses.

Financial cushion: what you need to keep yourself sane when business is slow. The more money you have in your emergency savings fund, the better.

Financial statements: documents consisting primarily of your monthly profit and loss, and your monthly balance sheet. These two documents lay out the health of your business in a way that nothing else can.

Income statement: a record of the total income and expenses for your business over a period of time—usually a month, but often a quarter, and a year. The income statement from each current month must always be compared with previous months to determine trends and help diagnose problems.

Marketing angle: the key to your PMA campaign. In four words, it is *why you are different* or your competitive edge. *(See PMA.)*

Marketing mix: the magic combination of marketing tools that together create a seamless funnel of clients racing to purchase your services. This magic mix is not something you will determine overnight, and it often will change as you expand.

Marketing plan: the second key to your PMA campaign, it is how you share your marketing angle with your target market.

Motivational coach: someone who masterfully and enthusiastically combines the roles of consultant, coach, and psychologist, helping clients to think bigger, perform better, and feel more confident about themselves.

Multiple streams of income: a term popularized by the book of the same name by Robert Allen. As a coach, you're missing out if you only make money through coaching. The idea is to create various books, products, online packages, etc. that provide income to you even when you are *not* coaching. The more ways you can capitalize on your expertise, the better.

Perception: how people see you and your business based on your marketing efforts and success as a coach.

PMA: publicity, marketing, and advertising—all three of which together are the bedrock of whether potential clients find out about you, and ultimately decide to contact you.

Psychologist: someone who is licensed by the state to counsel individuals and/or groups on matters of mental health and well being.

Referrals: the best way to get new clients. So tell *everyone* you know about what you do, and tell them to spread the word!

Role model: what you need to be for your clients. In other words, you need to walk the walk and not just talk the talk. Be their guiding light, always.

Training: the classes, seminars, books, and hour spent establishing your skills and expertise as a coach.

Target market: the people to whom you are marketing your services; the more specific, the better.

Index